AQA GCSE

ENGLISH AND ENGLISH LANGUAGE

REVISION WORKBOOK
Foundation

Esther Menon   Consultant: **Peter Buckroyd**

D1344802

Heinemann

Part of Pearson

Heinemann is an imprint of Pearson Education Limited, Edinburgh Gate, Harlow, Essex, CM20 2JE.

www.pearsonschoolsandcolleges.co.uk

Heinemann is a registered trademark of Pearson Education Limited

Text © Pearson Education Limited 2011
Edited by Vicky Butt
Designed and Produced by Karnae Design, Oxford
Cover design by Wooden Ark Studios
Picture research by Elena Wright
Cover photo/illustration © Nikreates/Alamy
Printed in Malaysia, KHL-CTP

First published 2011

15 14 13
10 9 8 7 6 5 4

British Library Cataloguing in Publication Data
A catalogue record for this book is available from the British Library

ISBN 978 0 435 02726 1

Acknowledgements

The author and publisher would like to thank the following individuals and organisations for permission to reproduce copyright material:

P4 'Inheritance Tax' leaflet extract from the RSPCA. Reproduced with permission of the RSPCA. P6 Facebook extract from 'Countryside Alliance: Repeal the Hunting Act – Official Countryside Alliance Group'. Reproduced by permission of the Countryside Alliance. P22 'Eddie Izzard: Marathon Man' article. Reproduced by kind permission of Comic Relief. Copyright © Comic Relief 2010. Registered charity 326568 (England/Wales); SC039730 (Scotland). P28 Anti-Social Behaviour poster. Reproduced with permission of the Thames Valley Police. P28 Vandalism poster. Reproduced with permission of the Thames Valley Police. P37 Extract from 'Five Hours of Sport a Week for Every Child' from the Department for Children, Schools and Families. Crown Copyright material is reproduced by the permission of the Controller of HMSO and Queen's Printer for Scotland. P48 Article 'Shark Tales in South Africa' by Kevin Rushby, from The Guardian, 27 February 2010. Copyright © The Guardian News & Media Ltd. 2010. Reproduced with permission. P60 Advert 'Hello Boys' by The Autism Trust. Reproduced with permission of The Autism Trust. P61 Press release from The Autism Trust. Reproduced with permission of The Autism Trust. P81 Witney Firewalkers Transcript of Witney Firewalking Event. Reproduced by permission of Phototechniques Ltd. P88 'Suits Under Scrutiny' article. Reproduced with permission of Which.co.uk. P92 'Green Gym' leaflet. Used with permission of BTCV. P90 'Renault's Cool Wind of Change' article by Nat Barnes, 10th July 2010 from www. express.co.uk.

The author and publisher would like to thank the following individuals and organisations for permission to reproduce photographs:

P14 Kobal Collection Ltd: Walt Disney Pictures; P22 Rex Features: Alfie Hitchcock; P36 Getty Images: Alistair Berg; P47 Alamy Images: Stephen Frink Collection; P48 Alamy Images: Stephen Frink Collection; P70 Alamy Images: LOOK Die Bildagentur der Fotografen GmbH; P75 Getty Images: Barcroft Media; P80 Phototechniques Ltd; P82 Phototechniques Ltd; P85 Phototechniques Ltd

Every effort has been made to contact copyright holders of material reproduced in this book. Any omissions will be rectified in subsequent printings if notice is given to the publishers.

Websites
Pearson Education Limited is not responsible for the content of any external internet sites. It is essential for tutors to preview each website before using it in class so as to ensure that the URL is still accurate, relevant and appropriate. We suggest that tutors bookmark useful websites and consider enabling students to access them through the school/college intranet.

Contents

Understanding and producing non-fiction texts – Reading

Understanding and producing non-fiction texts – Writing

Sample exam paper

Introduction

Introduction

This Student Workbook is designed to help you target your revision and improve your skills in AQA GCSE English/English Language.

Some students think that there is no need to revise for English/English Language. This is simply not true! You should revise for English/English Language as much as for any other subjects, particularly because entry for so many jobs or courses of study is dependent on how you do in your English and Maths GCSEs.

The more you revise and practise past paper questions, the more confident you will become in knowing:

- your strengths, weaknesses and skills to concentrate on
- what kind of questions to expect in the exam and how they are laid out
- how the examiner will be marking what you write.

How to improve your revision techniques

1 **Use the specialists.** The first thing to do is to make use of your own teacher as he/she is a very valuable resource! Listen carefully to all their revision tips in lesson time and maybe even jot down your own code or symbol for top tips that are relevant to you, to help you when you revisit your notes. Make sure you are clear about your own target areas and have discussed how to improve them with your teacher. If your teacher is running extra revision lessons make sure you attend them.

2 **Get organised!** So many students begin their revision at a disadvantage because their books, papers and materials are in a mess. Consider getting a folder or two and investing in a few highlighter pens. Spend half an hour sticking in loose sheets and organising your notes. And make sure you don't leave valuable revision notes on the desk in the classroom where the lesson took place! It might sound obvious, but a regular handful of students I have taught for revision lessons all around the country forget to take their useful papers and notes away with them.

3 **Know the exam paper.** Check that you are familiar with what the exam paper looks like, how many marks are awarded for each question and how much you will be expected to write in your answer booklet. Work out how much time you should be spending on each answer and try to stick with that when you are doing practice papers.

4 **Discipline yourself to use a clear revision space.** When you are ready to revise, find a quiet area away from any distractions and don't fool yourself that browsing the Internet or staring at a computer screen or book is effective revision. Remember to take regular breaks and pace yourself. It is difficult to maintain your concentration span for very long periods of time. Breaking your revision into manageable sessions is much more worthwhile.

5 **Use a revision checklist.** For example, use the Revision planner on page ix of this Workbook. This could be a starting point for you to find out exactly what you know already and help you find any gaps in your knowledge. It should keep you focused on the areas you need to revise, rather than just concentrating on the ones you find easiest or most enjoyable.

6 **Revise actively.** The most effective way to revise is through active strategies; these involve writing and thinking rather than just staring at a book or screen. This means that you practise the skills you have studied, take part in completing revision activities and compare your answers with sample answers to see where you can improve your performance. Remember to use a clock to time yourself and keep up the pressure, just like in the exam room.

7 **Read!** Use a little of your leisure time to read texts from a variety of media, for example a broadsheet and a tabloid newspaper and adverts in magazines. Absorb the main story and viewpoint of any article. Notice some of the features that you will need to consider in the exam, such as main and supporting points, presentational features, intended audience and language.

8 **Check your work.** Read what you have written so that you can 'hear it aloud' in your head. Check that it makes sense. This is most certainly the 'boring bit' and many students fail to be disciplined to do this in the exam. But for many of you working at the borderline between two grades, this strategy can mean the difference between one grade and the next.

Revision checklist

How confident do you feel about each of the areas that you need to revise for your exam? Fill in the revision checklist below.

▶ Tick green if you feel confident about this topic.

▶ Tick amber if you know some things, but revision will help improve your knowledge and skills to the best they can be.

▶ Tick red if you are not confident about two or more aspects of this topic.

Section	Revision lesson (60–90 minutes)	Where to find more information to improve my skills	Improving my responses	R	A	G
Reading	**IF** Identifying and commenting on audience and purpose	**2** Read and understand texts: purpose and audience	I can identify an audience of a text.			
			I can identify more than one audience of a text.			
			I can identify the purpose of a text.			
			I can identify more than one purpose of a text.			
			I can select relevant evidence to prove my answer.			
			I can comment on the evidence I have selected.			
Reading	**2F** Using evidence to support your points	**I** Read and understand texts: finding information	I can understand an unfamiliar text after reading it on my own.			
			I understand the meaning of the term 'viewpoint'.			
			I can work out the viewpoint being conveyed in a text.			
			I can select relevant evidence that shows the writer's viewpoint.			
			I can comment on evidence to justify my conclusions.			
Reading	**3F** Approaching the longer Reading questions	**3** Read and understand texts: argument, fact and opinion	I can identify the range of devices used by writers to achieve effects in a text.			
			I can select relevant evidence to prove my answer.			
			I can comment on the evidence I have selected.			
			I can identify a series of separate relevant points in answer to longer Reading questions.			

Section	Revision lesson (60–90 minutes)	Where to find more information to improve my skills	Improving my responses	R	A	G
Reading	4F Comparing and cross-referencing texts	7 Collate and compare	I can compare two or more texts': • content • audience • purpose • language features • presentational and structural features.			
			I can find evidence to support my opinions on the above.			
			I can explain the similarities and differences I have identified.			
Writing	5F Organising your ideas for writing	9 Organise information and ideas	I can plan a series of points.			
			I discipline myself **always** to make a plan before I write.			
			I can sequence my planned points in a logical order.			
			I can structure and paragraph my writing to reflect my plan.			
Writing	6F Using a range of vocabulary and sentence forms	10 Use language and structure	I can consistently write in sentences that are complete and grammatically correct.			
			I understand the terms simple, complex, compound and minor sentences.			
			I can write in simple, complex, compound and minor sentences.			
			I can choose particular sentence types to achieve particular effects in my writing.			
			I can choose vocabulary to create particular effects in my writing.			

Section	Revision lesson (60–90 minutes)	Where to find more information to improve my skills	Improving my responses	R	A	G
Writing	**7F** Using a variety of punctuation	**I1** Use and adapt forms	I can use commas, full stops, question marks, ellipses and exclamation marks.			
			I can punctuate direct speech correctly.			
			I remember to use a variety of punctuation marks in my writing.			
Writing	**8F** Proofreading	**I2** Use accurate punctuation	I can recognise when sentences are secure or insecure.			
			I can use a range of punctuation accurately.			
			I can use a range of vocabulary that is accurately spelt.			
			I always proofread my written work.			
Writing	**9F** Writing to communicate effectively	**I4** Use a range of sentence structures	I can identify the text type, audience and purpose required of a Writing exam question.			
			I can write in a variety of forms and include their appropriate presentational, structural and language features.			
			I can identify an appropriate register (when to write formally and when to write informally).			

Revision planner

Your school may advise you on how to use a revision planner or even provide you with a schedule. Of course you will need to plan your English revision within a sensible schedule of revision for all your subjects.

You might like to use the template below to map out the time you will spend on each subject. This will help you discipline yourself to cover **all** subjects; we all tend to focus on what we enjoy and avoid what we find difficult! You might find it helpful to alternate revision of a subject you like, with one you find less enjoyable. Remember to plan in some treats and relaxation as well.

	WEEK 1	WEEK 2	WEEK 3	WEEK 4	WEEK 5	WEEK 6	WEEK 7	WEEK 8	EXAM DATE
Reading:									
IF Identifying and commenting on audience and purpose									
2F Using evidence to support your points									
3F Approaching the longer Reading questions									
4F Comparing and cross-referencing texts									
Writing:									
5F Organising your ideas for writing									
6F Using a range of vocabulary and sentence forms									
7F Using a variety of punctuation									
8F Proofreading									
9F Writing to communicate effectively									

What your GCSE exam paper looks like

Centre number					Candidate number	
Surname						
Other names						
Candidate signature						

AQA

General Certificate of Secondary Education
Foundation Tier

English/English Language

ENG 1F
F

Unit 1 Understanding and producing non-fiction texts

Time allowed

The front cover will always remind you about how long you have to complete the whole paper (2 hours)

• 2 hours 15 minutes

Instructions

• Use black ink or black ball-point pen.

• Fill in the boxes at the top of this page.

Make sure you answer ALL of the questions

• Answer **all** questions.

• You must answer the questions in the spaces provided. Do not write outside the box around each page or on blank pages.

• Do all rough work in this book. Cross through any work you do not want to be marked.

Check your answers carefully before the end of the exam because marks on each question are given for sentence structure, punctuation and spelling

• You must refer to the insert provided.

• You must **not** use a dictionary.

Information

• The marks for questions are shown in brackets.

• The maximum mark for this paper is 80.

The marks for Section A and Section B are equal so you should divide your time equally between the two sections (about 1 hour on each section)

• There are 40 marks for Section A and 40 marks for Section B.

• You are reminded of the need for good English and clear presentation in your answers.

• You will be assessed on the quality of your reading in Section A.

• You will be assessed on the quality of your writing in Section B.

Advice

• You are advised to spend about one hour on Section A and one hour on Section B.

Using the Workbook

This Student Workbook has been written to help you to revise the skills and knowledge that you have covered in your AQA GCSE English and English Language course.

The Workbook has been designed for you to revise *actively*. There is plenty of room for you to write answers to the activities and practice exam questions. Throughout, you are encouraged to highlight and annotate exam questions and texts as you will in the exam.

Every lesson will open with an **Improving my responses** table. You need to decide how confident you are with each of the skills listed. You can record your confidence using a traffic light system. The lesson then goes over these skills and at the end of the lesson you review your confidence. Hopefully your knowledge of the skills will have improved.

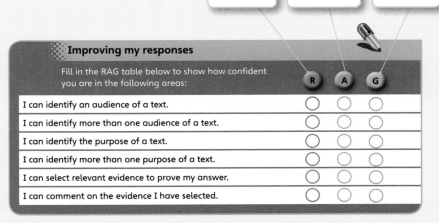

Red: I am not confident

Amber: I am semi-confident

Green: I am confident

Improving my responses

Fill in the RAG table below to show how confident you are in the following areas:

	R	A	G
I can identify an audience of a text.	○	○	○
I can identify more than one audience of a text.	○	○	○
I can identify the purpose of a text.	○	○	○
I can identify more than one purpose of a text.	○	○	○
I can select relevant evidence to prove my answer.	○	○	○
I can comment on the evidence I have selected.	○	○	○

Each activity suggests how much time you should spend on it. This is for guidance only. Where you answer an exam-style question, the suggested timing will be linked to how much time you will have in the actual exam to answer this type of question.

10 minutes

Each lesson has an **Improving my responses** activity. In these activities you will practise the specific skills that you have revised in the lesson and try to improve a lower grade answer by one grade. This Workbook focuses on the Foundation tier, so you will be looking at E–C grades.

At the end of each lesson there is a **GradeStudio** section. This gives you the opportunity to read examiner comments and grade criteria and match these to example student answers. This exam work should help you understand how to improve your responses.

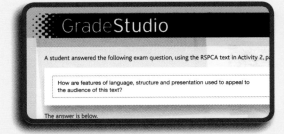

GradeStudio

A student answered the following exam question, using the RSPCA text in Activity 2, p...

How are features of language, structure and presentation used to appeal to the audience of this text?

The answer is below.

You can find answers to the activities online.

Good luck with your revision. As you begin the final countdown towards your exams, get ready to focus on skills and feel your confidence improve!

Identifying and commenting on audience and purpose

Skills you need:

You must show that you can:
- Identify the purpose(s) of a text
- Identify the audience(s) of a text
- Establish how a text's content is linked to audience and purpose

Before you answer questions on any Reading text in the exam, you must stop and identify the **audience** and **purpose** of the text. Sometimes a text can have more than one audience and purpose.

You will also need to be clear **what kind of text** it is and its **source** (where it is from) if possible. This knowledge will provide a firm

anchor for any of your comments about the text you have read.

In this lesson we will practise identifying audience (who a text is written for, e.g. children, taxi drivers) and its purpose (what a text is for and what effect it should have on its audience, e.g. to inform, to entertain).

Improving my responses

Fill in the RAG table below to show how confident you are in the following areas:

	R	A	G
I can identify an audience of a text.	◯	◯	◯
I can identify more than one audience of a text.	◯	◯	◯
I can identify the purpose of a text.	◯	◯	◯
I can identify more than one purpose of a text.	◯	◯	◯
I can select relevant evidence to prove my answer.	◯	◯	◯
I can comment on the evidence I have selected.	◯	◯	◯

Activity 1

10 minutes

Identify the correct audience and purpose for each extract in the table on page 3. Select the correct word or words from the banks below and write your answer in the table.

Audience

Young children	Home Internet users
Pregnant women	Rail users
Parents	Parents of young children
Householders	Users of public transport
County Council	The general public

Purpose

To entertain	To review
To persuade	To argue
To comment	To analyse
To inform	To advise

	Extract	Audience(s)	Purpose(s)
1	I am disgusted by the poor service offered by your refuse collectors. The waste in West Riding has not been collected now for four weeks. This is beginning to encourage vermin.		
2	Have you considered changing your broadband provider? Phone us today and you could save your household up to £30 a month.		
3	Your child is eligible for the HINI swine flu vaccine. Please phone your local health centre to book an appointment. Evidence shows that children under five are most seriously affected by the HINI virus and hospitalisation is a serious risk.		
4	Mrs Penn was going to have her new baby. Granny and granddad had come to stay to look after the twins while Mr and Mrs Penn went to the hospital.		
5	Your table is reserved. The wine is chilled. Sit back and let us serve you as you enjoy a leisurely journey to your destination by the Royal Dernford railway.		
6	Eating raw or partially cooked eggs during pregnancy presents a risk of listeria. We therefore suggest that you ensure all yolks are fully cooked.		
7	The décor was modern and stylish. The ambience second to none. There is no doubt that the 'Koh in Nor' is a jewel in the crown of Gloucestershire eateries.		

Activity 2

20 minutes

I Read the text below and establish the TAPS (see table opposite) of this leaflet.

INHERITANCE TAX

A legacy to the RSPCA saves and protects animals.

Inheritance tax is a tax on the value of a person's estate when they die and on certain gifts made by that person during their lifetime. The inheritance tax threshold is the amount above which inheritance tax becomes payable.

If you live in the United Kingdom, and the value of everything you own comes to more than £312,000 (inheritance tax threshold for the tax year 2008/2009), you may have to pay inheritance tax. This sum may sound like a lot, but once you take into account the value of your home plus any savings or insurance policies, you may find your estate is worth more than you realised.

You may not realise that inheritance tax can also apply to large gifts you may have made within the seven years before your death.

However, these are the main ways to make sure you won't have to pay this tax.

- If you are married, anything you leave to your spouse remains untaxed (although their own estate, which includes their inheritance from you, may be taxed in its own right when they die).

- Anything you leave to charity is paid free of inheritance tax. These gifts are taken out of your estate before any tax is worked out, so there may be times when a gift to charity could substantially reduce the tax your estate pays — or even remove it altogether.

- There are different tax levels for different types of large gifts you may have made before you died. You may want to speak to your solicitor about this.

The figure we have given above for the inheritance tax threshold was correct at time of printing. You should always speak to a solicitor about tax planning as there may be help available to you.

If you decide to include the RSPCA in your will, you don't need to tell us — we understand that it is a very personal and private matter. However, it will help us if you are prepared to let us know your decision, in absolute confidence.

The aims of the RSPCA are to prevent cruelty and promote kindness to animals.
The RSPCA is a charity registered in England and Wales. Registered Charity no. 219099

TAPS

Text type	Audience	Purpose	Source

2 Here is a list of features we might expect to find in a non-fiction text. Which of these would you expect to find in a text with the TAPS you have identified above?

Features of language, structure and presentation	Tick or cross
Bullet points	
Title/Heading	
Subtitle	
Formal language	
Informal language	
Images	
Captions	
Slang	
Simple sentences	
Complex sentences	
Compound sentences	
Imperative verbs	
Logo	
Specialist legal vocabulary	
Emotive language	
Mainly facts	
Mainly opinions	
Clichés	
Similes	
Lots of descriptive language	
Nouns	
Use of the first-person plural 'we'	
Specialist political vocabulary	
Rhetorical questions	

3 Now find examples of these features in the leaflet on page 4. Annotate the leaflet to mark these features. Has the charity used the features you were expecting to find?

Activity 3

20 minutes

1 Read the text below, then establish the TAPS of this extract.

---

facebook   Home   Profile   Account ▾

COUNTRYSIDE ALLIANCE

Love the countryside

Repeal the Hunting Act – official Countryside Alliance Group

Wall   **Info**   Discussions   Photos

Basic Info

Basic Info

Name: Repeal the Hunting Act – official Countryside Alliance Group

Category: Common Interest – Politics

Description: This group has been created for facebook members to show their support for the repeal of the Hunting Act.

WHY?

Repealing against a pointless, prejudiced and failed law.

The Hunting Act is unique in that its effects are entirely negative. It diminishes respect for Parliament, it puts law-abiding people at risk of prosecution, it diverts police attention from real crime, it brings no benefit to the environment, it is a blatant example of political prejudice and it does nothing for the welfare or conservation of the species it claims to 'protect'.

To achieve repeal and safeguard the future of hunting it is vital that we are able to grow our strength in numbers and resolve. Repeal cannot be taken for granted and each and every one of us must pledge ourselves to, and work for, the repeal of this flawed Act.

HOW?

Scrapping the Act need not be complicated or time consuming. In fact, it could be remarkably simple. The Alliance's campaign has seen public and political support for the Act fall dramatically and it seems more and more likely that a future Parliament will have a majority of MPs who support its repeal. Meanwhile, David Cameron has consistently repeated the Conservative manifesto commitment for a free vote on repeal followed by a Government Bill in Government time to get rid of it.

WHEN?

Hunting has survived the initial impact of the Hunting Act with its infrastructure largely intact, but only because of the determination of the hunting community and the realistic possibility of repeal. A new Government after the next Election could offer an opportunity which will never be repeated. The Alliance must be ready and able to close the deal on repeal for the good of hunting and all other rural activities.

Recent news

News: Dear All

Fighting for repeal and for the countryside.

Within the next 15 months there will be a General Election that will be critical to the future of hunting, the countryside, country pursuits and the rural way of life.

We could be on the verge of real and lasting change in the way governments deal with the countryside. Furthermore, we are the only organisation campaigning for repeal of the Hunting Act. Repeal would be a great victory in itself, but it would also protect all other country pursuits for a generation and open the way for policies that address the real needs of rural communities.

It has never been more important that the Countryside Alliance has the ability to influence public, political and media opinion.

This is why the Alliance is preparing the Rural Manifesto that will call on the next Government to:

• Repeal the Hunting Act and champion country pursuits

• Support British farmers and producers

• Enable all children to gain a practical understanding of the countryside

The Alliance has become one of the most lean and efficient, as well as Britain's best known and effective rural campaigning group. We are in tough economic times, but we need to raise our income. We cannot waste this unique opportunity to put the countryside at the heart of Government policy.

Please show your support for the Rural Manifesto, by joining this fan page

Many thanks, once again, for your continued support

The Countryside Alliance

TAPS

Text type	Audience	Purpose	Source

2   What are the appropriate features for such a text? Tick the appropriate language, structural and presentational features you would expect to find on a social networking page for the audience and purpose you have identified.

Features of language, structure and presentation	Tick or cross	Features of language, structure and presentation	Tick or cross
Bullet points		Logo	
Title/Heading		Specialist legal vocabulary	
Subtitle		Emotive language	
Formal language		Mainly facts	
Informal language		Mainly opinions	
Images		Clichés	
Captions		Similes	
Slang		Extensive descriptive language	
Simple sentences		Nouns	
Complex sentences		Use of the first person plural 'we'	
Compound sentences		Specialist political vocabulary	
Imperative verbs		Rhetorical questions	

3   Now find examples of these features in the web page on page 6. Annotate the web page to mark these features. Has the group used the features you were expecting to find?

Activity 4

I Now look at the student responses to the question below. These are exam responses identifying and commenting on audience and purpose. The students should be using 'point, evidence, explanation' (PEE) to structure their answers.

Identify the point, evidence and explanation in each student response by highlighting them in pink (point), yellow (evidence) and green (explanation).

How are features of language, structure and presentation used to appeal to the audience of this text? **(12 marks)**

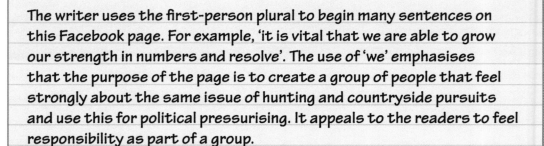

Student A

The writer uses the first-person plural to begin many sentences on this Facebook page. For example, 'it is vital that we are able to grow our strength in numbers and resolve'. The use of 'we' emphasises that the purpose of the page is to create a group of people that feel strongly about the same issue of hunting and countryside pursuits and use this for political pressurising. It appeals to the readers to feel responsibility as part of a group.

Student B

'We' is used in this article because it makes everyone feel involved. It makes readers feel like the page is written for them because they are interested in hunting. It helps them to be part of a group which is what Facebook is for, to make groups of people come together.

2 Decide which paragraph is likely to achieve a D grade and which is likely to achieve a C grade based on the following criteria.

D
▶ **Attempts to engage with task**
▶ **Identifies audience**
▶ **Some evidence of supporting detail**

C
▶ **Clear attempt to engage with task**
▶ **Identifies audience supported by clear evidence and comment**

3 Now write your own paragraph on a feature you identified in the Facebook text in Activity 3, question 2. Use the PEE structure and make links with the audience and purpose in your explanation.

A student answered the following exam question, using the RSPCA text in Activity 2, page 4.

> How are features of language, structure and presentation used to appeal to the audience of this text?
>
> (12 marks)

The answer is below.

You need to identify the weaknesses in this student answer. You should:

- list the improvements you would suggest
- rewrite the student answer to improve it.

Extract typical of a C grade answer

Clear:

This information leaflet is written for old people.

One idea the writer uses is simple sentences. This makes the information easy for the reader to read.

Another idea is it uses the word 'you' to write to the reader and make them feel involved in the information.

It also uses bullet points to show the different ways of getting out of inheritance tax.

Informative:

The information in this leaflet is written for old people who are interested in the RSPCA.

One feature that is used is specialist vocabulary. Examples of this are The inheritance tax threshold is the amount above which inheritance tax becomes payable.

If you live in the United Kingdom, and the value of everything you own comes to more than £312,000 (inheritance tax threshold for the tax year 2008/2009), you may have to pay inheritance tax.

Another feature used is words like may, should and could. These are helpful to the reader in giving ideas about what to do with their money without sounding too pushy.

C
- ▶ Clearly linked to the question
- ▶ Includes relevant features of language, presentation and structure
- ▶ Gives several different points about audience with evidence and comment

Suggestions for improvement

_____

_____

_____

_____

_____

Improved answer

_____

_____

_____

_____

_____

Improving my responses

Now that you have completed this lesson on audience and purpose, fill in the RAG table below to see if your confidence has improved.

	R	A	G
I can identify an audience of a text.	○	○	○
I can identify more than one audience of a text.	○	○	○
I can identify the purpose of a text.	○	○	○
I can identify more than one purpose of a text.	○	○	○
I can select relevant evidence to prove my answer.	○	○	○
I can comment on the evidence I have selected.	○	○	○

2F / Using evidence to support your points

Skills you need:

You must show that you can:
- Understand what a text is about
- Understand the viewpoint being conveyed by a text
- Select relevant evidence to support your conclusions
- Comment on that evidence

You will have read a range of texts in your English lessons. Often you will have established the main argument within a text with the help of your teacher. In the exam, you must make sure you understand the meaning and point of view conveyed by a text before you begin writing about it.

In this lesson you will practise identifying the writer's point of view and choosing quotations that prove this.

Improving my responses

Fill in the RAG table below to show how confident you are in the following areas:

	R	A	G
I can understand an unfamiliar text after reading it on my own.	○	○	○
I understand the meaning of the term 'viewpoint'.	○	○	○
I can work out the viewpoint being conveyed in a text.	○	○	○
I can select relevant evidence that shows the writer's viewpoint.	○	○	○
I can comment on evidence to justify my conclusions.	○	○	○

Activity 1

10 minutes

On the ratings chart opposite, write the titles of **three different** text types about which you have a viewpoint. You could include a book, a film, a TV programme or a computer game. Add one that you dislike, one that you judge as average and one that you rate highly.

Under each title, fill in the box to justify your viewpoint giving a clear reason and evidence from the examples you have chosen.

For example:

'I rate this text as ...
My reason for this is ...'

Remind yourself of the meaning of the terms 'viewpoint' and 'evidence'.

Viewpoint is: a person or organisation's mental attitude towards a topic.

Evidence is: the proof that can support a conclusion/viewpoint.

An example has been done for you:

Title: Ghost Manor

Book

I rate this book as excellent.

My reason for this is that it is extremely spooky. The setting adds to this and I can imagine the gloomy building where the events happen.

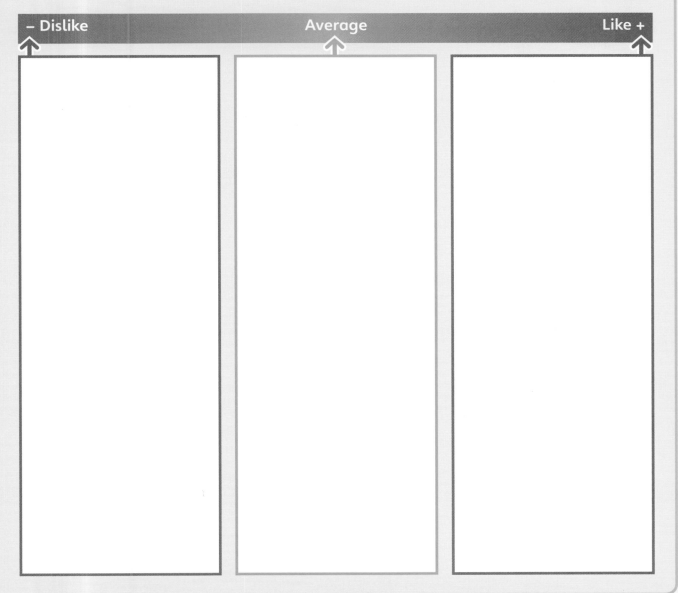

– Dislike	Average	Like +

Activity 2

15 minutes

1 Look at this still image selected from the *Alice in Wonderland* 2010 movie trailer. Now watch the trailer, which you can access by going to www.imdb.com and typing 'Alice in Wonderland 2010' into the search box at the top of the web page.

2 Choose **two** of the viewpoints from the list below and select evidence from the still image and trailer to prove them. Comment on how the evidence justifies that viewpoint.

● The quality of the special effects is spectacular.

● The surreal movie set creates a dream-like quality.

● It is rightly full of colourfully eccentric characters.

● It is full of humour through the actions and dialogue of the characters.

Viewpoint I: _____

_____

Evidence to support it: _____

_____

_____

Explanation: _____

_____

_____

Viewpoint 2: _____

_____

Evidence to support it: _____

_____

_____

Explanation: _____

_____

_____

3 Read part of an example answer below. The student has used point , evidence and explanation to establish their viewpoint. You must remember to use this format in your answers to Reading questions.

> The quality of the special effects is spectacular. One particular example of this is scene in the trailer showing the armies of playing cards, white and red, marching to battle. The special effects make it clear that these are playing cards, while at the same time making them look threatening and alive as warriors.

Activity 3

1 Read this film review.

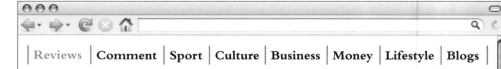

| Reviews | Comment | Sport | Culture | Business | Money | Lifestyle | Blogs |

Alice in Wonderland

IF ANYONE was born to make <u>Alice In Wonderland</u> it was Tim Burton.

Over the past quarter of a century Burton has beguiled us with dazzling flights of fancy that have revealed the eye of a painter, the bravado of a showman and the tender heart of a true romantic.

He should have been perfect for the task but there is something about this 3-D Alice that doesn't quite work.

You certainly cannot fault the production design. It is as if Salvador Dali had been let loose to create a Wonderland of gnarled tree stumps, ruined castles and the charred remains of happier days.

The special effects are adequate, although it is plain to see that poor Alice (Mia Wasikowska) is battling with thin air during the film's climactic duel.

The real problem is the tone of the film as Burton provides oodles of eccentricity but little in the way of enchantment.

Alice is now 19 and facing the unbearable stress of a wedding proposal that she dare not refuse. No wonder she falls down a rabbit hole into a strangely familiar world. A 'drink me' potion makes her shrink. An 'eat me' cake transforms her into a giant but it all seems too confusing for her.

'You'd think she would remember all this from the last time,' sighs the Dodo Bird (voiced by Michael Gough) and you can't help but agree.

The older Alice is reunited with many of her former acquaintances as she discovers that her true destiny is to fight the Jabberwocky (voiced by Christopher Lee) and free everyone from the tyrannical reign of the Red Queen (Helena Bonham Carter).

It can't have taken a huge stretch of the imagination to devise a story like that. Quite what everyone has been doing for the past 13 years, apart from awaiting Alice's return, is one of the questions that the perfunctory plot chooses not to address.

This version of Alice does have some fun moments as Helena Bonham Carter's imperious Queen rests her feet on a warm pig's belly or Matt Lucas rolls into sight as Tweedledum and Tweedledee looking for all the world like two potatoes who have fallen from a sack.

Vocal talents are well-matched with the Lewis Carroll characters, as Stephen Fry voices the silky Cheshire Cat and Alan Rickman's velvety tones can be heard behind the Blue Caterpillar.

The animated creatures and live action performers don't always make for the smoothest blend and Johnny Depp's Mad Hatter is one of the disappointments.

Decked out in carrot-coloured wig, Depp's character seems genuinely deranged as his voice slides between lisping and loopy to the sinister growl of a Glasgow hard man after a night on the town.

Depp is game for anything but it almost seems as if he just threw everything at the character (silly accents, an even sillier dance, a tipsy hint of Jack Sparrow, etc) and his old collaborator Tim Burton never made up his mind what to do with all that energy and invention.

Burton's *Alice In Wonderland* joins the ranks of *Return To Oz* and *Hook* in confirming that it's rarely a good idea to return to the scene of a classic novel unless you have something new and exciting to bring. Alice is certainly diverting but it is far from the important date that it might have been.

Reviewed by Allan Hunter

VERDICT 3/5   **(Cert PG; 107mins)**

2 Underline and annotate the film review to help you answer this two-part exam question:

> **a) What reasons can you find in the review for saying that Burton's film is impressive?**
>
> **b) What reasons can you find in the review for saying that Burton's film is disappointing?**   **(8 marks)**

You may find it useful to use one colour for the reasons you find for part a) and a different colour for part b).

Activity 4   **5 minutes**

Summarise, in **one** sentence, the overall viewpoint of the reviewer on this film.

_____

_____

_____

1 Suggest how you can improve the answer below. Part a) and b) of the exam question from page 17 has been split into two parts.

> b) What reasons can you find in the review for saying that Burton's film is disappointing?

Student answer

One reason the reviewer says the film is bad is that he thinks noone should make a version of a classic novel. He says 'it's rarely a good idea to return to the scene of a classic novel'. He also thinks it is bad because the Mad Hatter who is Johnny Depp is too stupid. I thought he was good and his costume was excellent.
Another reason why he criticises it is because the special effects were only OK.

- ▶ Some evidence that the text is understood
- ▶ Attempts to engage with the text and make inferences (come to conclusions)
- ▶ Offers some relevant quotation to support what has been understood
- ▶ Makes some reference to events and ideas in the text

- ▶ Clear evidence that the text is understood
- ▶ Engages with the text and makes inferences (comes to conclusions)
- ▶ Offers relevant and appropriate quotation
- ▶ Interprets the text and makes connections between events and ideas

Suggestions for improvement

_____

_____

_____

_____

_____

Improved answer

_____

_____

_____

_____

_____

2 Consider the following answer to the other part of the question. Annotate the script to show where the student has identified and used evidence in their response.

> a) What reasons can you find in the review for saying that Burton's film is impressive?

Although he criticises the film in many ways there are things the reviewer says are good. The reviewer praises the use of the actors in the film and the way their voices have been well-matched with the characters in the film. For example, he mentions that the actors speaking the parts of the Cheshire Cat and the blue caterpillar work well. The words 'silky' and 'velvety tones' praise the way the voices and images work well.

He also thinks there is humour and fun in the film. 'Matt Lucas rolls into sight as Tweedledum and Tweedledee'. This would be funny to see people in *Alice in Wonderland* who actually look a bit like modern celebrities. He says production design is OK and talks about the woods and castles on the screen being good.

Improving my responses

Now that you have completed this lesson on using evidence to support your points, fill in the RAG table below to see if your confidence has improved.

	R	A	G
I can understand an unfamiliar text after reading it on my own.	○	○	○
I understand the meaning of the term 'viewpoint'.	○	○	○
I can work out the viewpoint being conveyed in a text.	○	○	○
I can select relevant evidence that shows the writer's viewpoint.	○	○	○
I can comment on evidence to justify my conclusions.	○	○	○

3F Approaching the longer Reading questions

Skills you need:

You must show that you can:
- Clearly understand a text and its features
- Select relevant and appropriate examples from the texts to support ideas
- Make enough separate points to demonstrate the above

The longer Reading question requires you to consider the way a text is built. It asks you to comment on this.

The longer Reading question is worth a lot of marks. You should look at how many marks are available for each exam question. You must make enough relevant points, with evidence from the text, to deserve full marks.

Make sure each of your points is different – of course you won't gain more marks for writing a longer answer that just repeats the same point! Think carefully about timing; you should spend three times longer on a 12-mark question than on a 4-mark question.

In this lesson you will:
- practise identifying the information conveyed in a text
- consider the language and devices the writer has chosen to use
- focus on making enough separate points for the marks available.

Improving my responses

Fill in the RAG table below to show how confident you are in the following areas:	R	A	G
I can identify the range of devices used by writers to achieve effects in a text.	○	○	○
I can select relevant evidence to prove my answer.	○	○	○
I can comment on the evidence I have selected.	○	○	○
I can identify a series of separate relevant points in answer to a longer Reading question.	○	○	○

Activity 1

Sort the phrases below into facts and opinions.

	Fact or opinion?
one of Britain's best-loved comedians, Eddie Izzard	
the ultimate challenge of human endurance	
43 marathons in 51 days	
it became all too clear that Eddie's body may not be able to sustain him	
Marathon Man, is a three-part documentary	
part one airing on BBC Three tonight	
the documentary gets to the painful heart of what drove him to achieve the seemingly impossible	
To really get to the heart of Eddie's challenge, tune in to BBC Three tonight	
in the summer of 2009	
Eddie, who'd never run a marathon before, gave himself just over five weeks to prepare	
Eddie said: 'It's been hell, 26 miles a day is a lot. Try that six times a week.'	
Eddie didn't give up	
he was joined by celebrities Frank Skinner and Denise Van Outen in Edinburgh	

Activity 2

1   Read the web page article on page 22 and establish the TAPS.

Text type = _____

Audience = _____

Purpose = _____

Source = _____

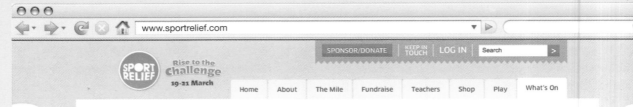

www.sportrelief.com

SPONSOR/DONATE | KEEP IN TOUCH | LOG IN | Search >

Home | About | The Mile | Fundraise | Teachers | Shop | Play | What's On

'Eddie Izzard: Marathon Man' on BBC Three tonight

4th Mar 2010

Last summer one of Britain's best-loved comedians, Eddie Izzard, completed the ultimate challenge of human endurance. He completed a staggering 43 marathons in 51 days around the UK for Sport Relief.

An inspiring and, at times, emotional journey of discovery was captured on film. *Eddie Izzard: Marathon Man*, is a three-part documentary following Eddie's epic endeavour, with part one airing on BBC Three tonight.

The series looks at how Eddie took on this gruelling feat for Sport Relief, covering a mind-blowing 1,166 miles. The documentary follows every step of the journey. It gets to the painful heart of what drove him to achieve the impossible. He struggled with and overcame the physical and mental battering from running consecutive marathons.

Professional athletes would struggle with this challenge, but Eddie, who'd never run a marathon before, gave himself just over five weeks to prepare. As the miles clocked up, it became clear that Eddie's body might not be able to sustain him as it came under attack from all sides.

Eddie endured a host of obstacles: bad weather conditions, tough terrain, crippling injuries, painful stomach problems from his extreme diet of over 6,000 calories a day, the tortuous daily routine of nightly ice baths and, to top it off, sleeplessness.

Eddie said: 'It's been hell, 26 miles a day is a lot. Try that six times a week. At first the last six miles were pure agony. Then it changed to the first six miles. Then it was the middle chunk. But now it's pretty much all the same. My feet are disintegrating, the small toes have lost their nails – they look like alien monsters but I'm told they will grow back. But I'll make it; my body isn't really determined but my brain is.'

Despite these mounting problems, Eddie didn't give up. He was rewarded for his herculean efforts with a special award at the 2009 BBC Sports Personality of the Year. To date he has raised over £300,000* for Sport Relief.

The documentary also meets the British public. They came out to give him their moral support sometimes in the most unlikely of places. It captures the moments when he was joined by celebrities **Frank Skinner** and **Denise Van Outen** in Edinburgh. A personal ice-cream van, playing the *Chariots of Fire* theme tune, accompanies Eddie throughout, spurring him on and collecting donations.

To really get to the heart of Eddie's challenge, tune in to BBC Three tonight at 10.30pm – and show Eddie your support by sponsoring him here!

* The broadcast of *Eddie Izzard: Marathon Man* on 4th March 2010 helped inspire donations that increased the amount raised by Eddie to £1.88 million.

2 Look at the question below. Notice that it asks you to identify two things: language to inform and language to persuade.

> **How does the web page use language to inform and persuade the reader? You could include:**
> • **details about Eddie's task and its difficulties**
> • **information about publicity and recognition by other celebrities**
> • **the final paragraph.** **(12 marks)**

Now skim and scan the first two paragraphs of the web page, underlining and points relevant to language to inform as you go.

3 Look at these PEE example answers about language to inform.

PEE example I:

> The first paragraph gives information about the challenge that Izzard took. '43 marathons in 51 days'… 'around the UK for Sport Relief'. The writer uses facts and figures to introduce what Izzard did, where he did it and why he did it.

PEE example 2:

> The web page goes on to give factual information about the TV programme that shows this. 'three-part documentary … with part one airing on BBC Three tonight.' The writer continues to use facts to give potential viewers information about where to find out more and when it is going to be shown on TV.

4 Now, skim and scan the rest of the article to underline as many relevant points about language to inform as you can.

23

Activity 3

Underline and annotate the sections of the Eddie Izzard text that answer the second part of the exam question below:

How does the web page use language to persuade the reader?

Write out your points in the space provided, using the PEE structure modelled on page 23.

Points:

The answer below needs more points to improve it. Write two or three additional PEE points to extend and improve the answer.

Extract typical of a C grade answer

> The web page also uses language to persuade the reader. Firstly it tries to persuade the reader that Izzard is a great man. It does this in the first paragraph by describing his celebrity status. 'one of Britain's best-loved comedians'. The adjective 'best loved' suggests that Izzard is extremely important and popular. It also uses opinions in the article to show how the challenge Izzard set himself was huge and difficult. For example it uses the word 'epic' which makes you think it was amazing and enormous what he did.'

Additional PEE points:

1 _____

_____

_____

2 _____

_____

_____

3 _____

_____

_____

Improving my responses

Now that you have completed this lesson on approaching the longer Reading questions, fill in the RAG table below to see if your confidence has improved.

	R	A	G
I can identify the range of devices used by writers to achieve effects in a text.	○	○	○
I can select relevant evidence to prove my answer.	○	○	○
I can comment on the evidence I have selected.	○	○	○
I can identify a series of separate relevant points in answer to a longer Reading question.	○	○	○

4F Comparing and cross-referencing texts

The AQA GCSE Foundation English paper asks you to read and answer questions on **three** different texts. It will also ask you to consider **two** of these together and look for similarities and differences. Many candidates who do not gain high marks write about one text and forget to write enough about the second.

This lesson will revise the different elements of a text that you might compare. It will also help you with planning an answer that deals with two texts at the same time. To gain the most marks in the exam you must think about similarities and differences and make comments that address *both* texts.

Improving my responses

Fill in the RAG table below to show how confident you are in the following areas:

	R	A	G
I can compare two or more texts':			
• content	○	○	○
• audience	○	○	○
• purpose	○	○	○
• language features	○	○	○
• presentational and structural features.	○	○	○
I can find evidence to support my opinions on the above.	○	○	○
I can explain the similarities and differences I have identified.	○	○	○

Remind yourself of the following terms and their meanings:

Collate means: _____

Compare means: _____

Activity 1

Sort the terms in the word bank into their relevant boxes.

To advise and inform	Lower case	Bold text
Rhetorical questions	Animal lovers	To persuade
Simple sentences	Font size	Short paragraphs
Compound sentences	Text boxes	Rhyme
To describe and entertain	Subheading	Headline
People interested in hunting	Byline	Imperatives
Specialist terminology, e.g. legal language	The elderly	Image
Parents with children	To comment	To inform
Use of colour	Teenagers	Caption
The general public	Upper case	To review
Potential criminals	Alliteration	Jobseekers

Audience – A

Purpose – P

Language features – L

Presentational and structural features – PS

Activity 2

20 minutes

1 Look at the two posters and identify the TAP of each one.

Text 1

Text 2

	Text type	Audience	Purpose
Text 1			
Text 2			

2 Look at the following exam question and underline any key terms.

> **Compare the two posters on the topic of anti-social behaviour.**
>
> **Use the headings below to structure your answer:**
> • **Content**
> • **Presentational and structural features**
> • **Language features.**
> (12 marks)

3 Look at the completed balloon plan below on the first bullet point 'Content'.

Then complete the other two planning balloons to answer the exam question.

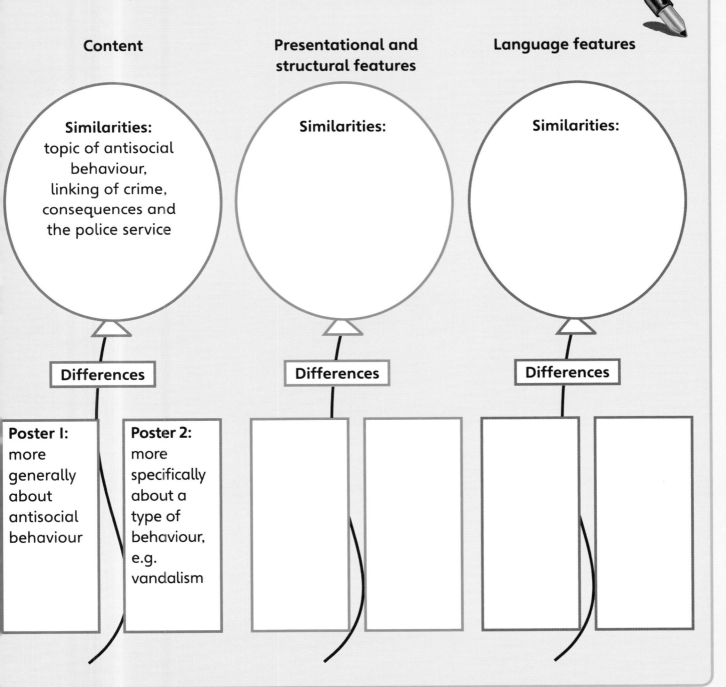

Content

Similarities:
topic of antisocial
behaviour,
linking of crime,
consequences and
the police service

Presentational and
structural features

Similarities:

Language features

Similarities:

Differences

Differences

Differences

Poster I:
more
generally
about
antisocial
behaviour

Poster 2:
more
specifically
about a
type of
behaviour,
e.g.
vandalism

Activity 3

20 minutes

Using your completed balloon planning diagram on page 29, complete an exam-style answer to the following question:

Compare the two posters on the topic of anti-social behaviour. Use the headings below to structure your answer:

• **Presentational and structural features**

• **Language features**

Continue ▸

Continue ▸

Activity 4

Now look at the grade criteria below. What grade do you think your answer from Activity 3 has achieved?

E
- ▶ Very few examples and not explained
- ▶ Limited comparison of the two texts
- ▶ Limited coverage of the three areas of language, presentational and structural features

D
- ▶ Identifies three or more features
- ▶ Some attempt to compare the texts
- ▶ Some evidence of proof/quotation and comment

C
- ▶ Clear attempt to engage with the activity
- ▶ A range of comparisons between the texts
- ▶ Language, presentational and structural features covered

Grade achieved: _____

Points for improvement: _____

_____

_____

_____

1 Read the sample student answer written in response to the exam question below.

> Compare the two posters on the topic of anti-social behaviour.
> Use the headings below to structure your answer:
> • Content
> • Presentational and structural features
> • Language features. (12 marks)

Student A

These two posters are both about anti-social behaviour. They are both put out by Thames Valley Police. They both have headlines which are warning about crimes (Anti-Social Behaviour' and 'Vandalism'). They are both unusual with graffiti and a till receipt.

2 Look at the criteria for an E grade answer and a C grade answer. Which grade do you think this answer would achieve and why?

- ▶ **Identification of at least two clear points**
- ▶ **Some comparison**
- ▶ **Deals with two bullets**

- ▶ **Clear and effective attempt to answer question**
- ▶ **Range of relevant points**
- ▶ **All three bullet points listed in the exam question covered**
- ▶ **Range of comparisons**

3 Try to improve the answer to reach your target grade, using the grade criteria on page 34.

_____
_____
_____
_____
_____
_____
_____
_____
_____
_____
_____
_____

Improving my responses

Now that you have completed this lesson on comparing and cross-referencing texts, fill in the RAG table below to see if your confidence has improved.

R   **A**   **G**

I can compare two or more texts':	R	A	G
• content	○	○	○
• audience	○	○	○
• purpose	○	○	○
• language features	○	○	○
• presentational and structural features.	○	○	○
I can find evidence to support my opinions on the above.	○	○	○
I can explain the similarities and differences I have identified.	○	○	○

5F / Organising your ideas for writing

Skills you need:

You must show that you can:
- Plan your writing
- Sequence information in paragraphs and as a complete text

You will have discussed the importance of planning Writing answers in your English lessons. But many students still fail to discipline themselves to do this in the exam.

The planning stage of writing is *crucial* for your success in the exam. How many times have you begun writing and then realised you have no idea how the piece will end? Good answers can be spoilt with a weak ending that just tails off. Answers which make one point of argument, and then just repeat the same point using slightly different words show an obvious lack of planning.

This lesson will focus on how to plan and order your points in response to a Writing question. It will support you in using a plan to make sure you paragraph your writing properly.

Improving my responses

Fill in the RAG table below to show how confident you are in the following areas:	R	A	G
I can plan a series of points.	○	○	○
I discipline myself **always** to make a plan before I write.	○	○	○
I can sequence my planned points in a logical order.	○	○	○
I can use my plan to structure and paragraph my writing.	○	○	○

Activity 1

10 minutes

1　Read the press report on the Government's policy on 5 hours of sport in schools, opposite.

FIVE HOURS OF SPORT A WEEK FOR EVERY CHILD

£100m CAMPAIGN, ANNUAL NATIONAL SCHOOL SPORTS WEEK ANNOUNCED

A £100m campaign to give every child the chance of five hours of sport every week was announced by the Prime Minister, Gordon Brown today.

He called for a 'united team effort' in the run up to 2012 to make sport a part of every child's day to build a greater sporting nation and a fitter nation. He wants schools, parents, volunteers, coaches and the sports world to offer the equivalent of an hour of sport to every child, every day of the school week.

The plans include greater emphasis on competition within and between schools, a network of competition managers and a new National School Sports Week.

The new funding will provide:

- up to five hours of sport per week for all pupils, including two hours within the curriculum, and three hours for young people aged 16–19
- a new National School Sport Week, championed by Dame Kelly Holmes where all schools will be encouraged to run sports days and inter-school tournaments. This will build on the success of the UK School Games and its impact on motivating young people to take part in competitive sport
- a network of 225 competition managers across the country to work with primary and secondary schools to increase the amount of competitive sport they offer
- more coaches in schools and the community to deliver expert sporting advice to young people.

The Government will also challenge the sporting bodies to develop modern school sport competitions leading to local, regional and national finals.

The new funding builds on the £633 million already committed to creating a world-class school sport and PE system over the next three years.

The Prime Minister said:

'We need to put school sport back where it belongs, playing a central role in the school day. I was lucky enough to have primary and secondary schools that had sport at the centre of their ethos. I want every child to have that opportunity to take part.

'Watching sport is a national pastime. Talking about sport is a national obsession. But now we need to make taking part in sport a national characteristic.

'Whatever their natural ability and whatever their age, sport and activity can make our children healthier, raise self-confidence and self-esteem. It develops teamwork, discipline and a sense of fair play. Values that will stand young people and the country in good stead in the years to come.

'To do this will take a concerted campaign, a real team effort. Government is doing its bit. Schools, parents, volunteers and the sporting world can do theirs. I call on them to join us. Together we can help every child be the best they can be.'

The moves will help strengthen the competitive framework for school sport – from grassroots to elite. The ultimate aim is for every child to have access to a range of sporting competition from local and regional level, leading on to national finals.

2 Three students answered the Writing question below.

> **Write a letter from a teenager to the Schools Minister, arguing for or against the policy of 5 hours of sport a week.** **(16 marks)**

Rank their answer openings from 1 to 3, with the best as number 1. The best answer should have the following:

- an interesting start
- appropriate register (formal/informal)
- a clear link to the question
- clarity for the reader/examiner about the audience and purpose of the text.

Student	Letter opening	Rank
Student A	Why are you doing it? It's unfair that we should all be made to do it. It's not everyone that likes getting sweaty and out of breath and lots of us are just not good at it and it makes people laugh at you.	
Student B	I am writing to you to about your press release about changes to sport in schools. I am disgusted about the new policy of five hours of compulsory sport. It seems as if there is one rule for adults and another for children. Do we see the politicians jogging round the House of Commons in their lunchtimes? Well, maybe only when they know the press is there to take a photo!	
Student C	It is about time that you did something about young people's health today. For lots of girls PE just aint happening and they need to diet. Reports show that many children are not eating healthily. It's time that things should change and it is the job of schools and parents to change things. I am glad that the government are doing something about it.	

Activity 2

5 minutes

What is the TAP of the text to be written by students in the exam question above?

Text type = _____

Audience = _____

Purpose = _____

Activity 3

20 minutes

1 Consider the exam question below and then look at the statements. You should plan an exam answer that argues *in support* of the policy of 5 hours of sport in schools.

> **Write a letter from a teenager to the Schools Minister, arguing for the policy of 5 hours of sport a week.** **(16 marks)**

Writing to argue needs to take **one** viewpoint but acknowledge a couple of opposing points of argument. For example, 'Some people argue there is just not enough time for sport in schools, but I think the timetable can always be adjusted to get rid of other less essential subjects.'

Choose **three** points of argument to support the policy and **two** from the opposing viewpoint that you will mention, but argue against. Use these to make a plan on page 40. You might like to do this in the form of a list or a spider diagram.

We are already doing more sport in schools than we were in 2008.
There is little enough time in schools to get through the requirements of GCSEs without adding more to lesson time.
There is not enough time for more PE in schools.
Today's children are just not fit enough and parents and schools need to do something about it.
Good health will have an impact on behaviour in schools.
Healthy children means happy children.
It is important to establish children having a lifelong love of sport.
Friendly competition is an important part of sport and an important part of life.
Sport can be offered not only in the curriculum but also for extra curricular or extended schools offerings.
Children today are less active than children of previous generations.
Obesity is an increasing problem in the UK so we need to begin a focus on health and fitness early in life.
Sport can give non-academic children an area in which to excel and gain respect.
Today's computer-generation children are becoming couch potatoes.

The statements from page 39 have been provided again for you on the opposite page.

Write your plan here:

2 Now write a similar plan arguing *against* the policy. In line with the process you followed for question 1, you should compose a long list of points, and then consider a five-point plan.

We are already doing more sport in schools than we were in 2008.

There is little enough time in schools to get through the requirements of GCSEs without adding more to lesson time.

There is not enough time for more PE in schools.

Today's children are just not fit enough and parents and schools need to do something about it.

Good health will have an impact on behaviour in schools.

Healthy children means happy children.

It is important to establish children having a lifelong love of sport.

Friendly competition is an important part of sport and an important part of life.

Sport can be offered not only in the curriculum but also for extra curricular or extended schools offerings.

Children today are less active than children of previous generations.

Obesity is an increasing problem in the UK so we need to begin a focus on health and fitness early in life.

Sport can give non-academic children an area in which to excel and gain respect.

Today's computer-generation children are becoming couch potatoes.

Activity 4

20 minutes

Now answer the exam-style question below using the plan you completed for Activity 3, question 2.

Write a letter from a teenager to the Schools Minister, arguing against the policy of 5 hours of sport a week. **(16 marks)**

Continue ▸

(lined answer space)

Activity 5

Look at the 'organisation of ideas' grade criteria below.

C
- ▶ **Clear identification with purpose and audience**
- ▶ **Begins to sustain reader's response**
- ▶ **Evidence of structure**
- ▶ **Usually coherent paragraphs/sections**
- ▶ **Clear selection of vocabulary for effect**

Have you addressed all of these points in your writing?

Look at your answer to Activity 4 in the light of this criteria and annotate one or two paragraphs with the changes you would make in order to improve it.

Read the conclusions from two student responses to the exam question below, together with the examiner comments. Then complete the Tips and practice section opposite.

> Write a letter from a teenager to the Schools Minister, arguing for or against the policy of 5 hours of sport a week.
>
> (16 marks)

Extract typical of a C grade answer

Student A

Effective vocabulary for a conclusion

Use of a variety of sentence structures

Appropriate sign off

Overall, I am very happy that the government is suggesting these changes. I will enjoy my new timetable and I am sure that other students who are less fit than me will gradually get better. While they might be reluctant at first, I hope this will help them stay fit as they grow up and maybe reduce the amount of illness and obesity amongst adults in this county. Let's hope for change!

Yours sincerely

Verbs that express viewpoint

Clear viewpoint maintained throughout

Use of short sentence for effect

Examiner comment

This is a secure piece of writing which demonstrates an awareness of audience and purpose and is appropriately formal. The student uses a secure vocabulary with some specialist terms. The letter ends neatly with a conclusion that links back to the question and maintains one viewpoint.

Extract typical of a D grade answer

Student B

Insecure punctuation insecure use of pronouns we/you.

Wrong sign off (should be 'Yours sincerely')

It is also important to remember that we should all have free choice. You aren't made to go running every morning so why should we. And while doctors say that exercise is good for you how many of them go get regular exercise. It's just adults telling you what to do. Why should we. Also the government are keen for standard to go up in schools. We can't do this while we are running around the cross country track.

Yours faithfully

Two different points of argument contained in the conclusion. No material that sums up the argument to conclude

Responds to issues but more appropriate for the body text than the conclusion

Tips and practice

Tips

Write down or discuss what you have learnt about:

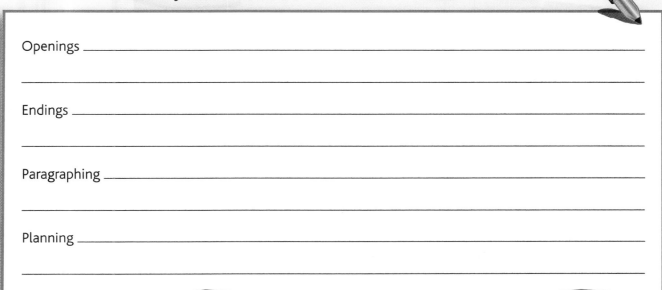

Openings _____

_____

Endings _____

_____

Paragraphing _____

_____

Planning _____

_____

Practice

Now you can apply what you have learnt to all your writing practice.

1 Plan your points.

2 Sequence your ideas.

3 Ensure your openings and endings are arresting and make explicit links to the key words in the title.

Improving my responses

Now that you have completed this lesson on organising your ideas for writing, it's time to fill in the RAG table below to see if your confidence has improved.

	R	A	G
I can plan a series of points.	○	○	○
I discipline myself **always** to make a plan before I write.	○	○	○
I can sequence my planned points in a logical order.	○	○	○
I can use my plan to structure and paragraph my writing.	○	○	○

Using a range of vocabulary and sentence forms

Skills you need:

You must show that you can:
- Write in secure sentences
- Use simple, compound, complex and minor sentences for effect
- Use a range of vocabulary for effect

To improve your responses to Writing questions you must show that you can use a range of sentence types and vocabulary. You need to choose vocabulary that is interesting and appropriate to your topic. Your response should show that you are aware of a reader and the effect of your text on that reader. For example, you may have been asked to inform, persuade or entertain your reader.

In this lesson you will:
- revise the different sentence types that you have learnt during your English course
- look at a model of writing where the author uses a variety of sentence structures to achieve particular effects
- put what you have seen into practice in your own writing.

Improving my responses

Fill in the RAG table below to show how confident you are in the following areas:	R	A	G
I can consistently write in sentences that are complete and grammatically correct.	○	○	○
I understand the terms simple, complex, compound and minor sentences.	○	○	○
I can write in simple, complex, compound and minor sentences.	○	○	○
I can choose particular sentence types to achieve particular effects in my writing.	○	○	○
I can choose vocabulary to create particular effects in my writing.	○	○	○

Activity 1

Look at the image. Then fill in the two word bank boxes below with language to convey the senses and specialist terms that might be associated with writing about this image.

Senses

salty water

Specialist terms

mask

Activity 2

I Read the article below, which is an extract from a longer text. As you read, underline any specialist/informative vocabulary and descriptive/entertaining language.

○○○

| Reviews | Comment | Sport | Travel | Business | Money | Lifestyle | Blogs |

Guardiantravel
Shark tales in South Africa

Scuba-diving with sharks in the Indian Ocean south of Durban, protected by just a mask and a wetsuit, rather than a steel cage.

I placed my mask over my face and checked the regulator. We had made it from the beach through the big surf – it was a rough day – and were now four miles off the South African coast, sitting on the gunwales of an inflatable dive boat that was rising and falling through two metres or more every few seconds.

'Remember,' said Kenny, one of the instructors, 'I'm your dive buddy – you stay with me. OK? If we see sharks, we remain calm, we stay upright in the water, we give them space.'

There is something quite comforting about the steady suck and hiss of Scuba apparatus. Your breathing slows and becomes regular. You are separated from the world by a sheet of glass. You get that irrational feeling of safety that a mosquito net can bring in man-eating lion territory.

And we were in man-eater country. The Indian Ocean coast of South Africa saw 86 shark attacks between 1992 and 2008, with 11 fatalities. Before the trip I went through the species of shark in my copy of *Sea Fishes of Southern Africa*, noting their characteristics: 'may threaten divers', 'positively linked to attacks on humans', 'voracious predator' – the word 'aggressive' came up time and again.

In Cape Town there is a much publicised thrill available whereby divers are lowered in a steel cage with some bait. Sharks then attack. Sharks, after all, are fiendishly dangerous. They are demons for a secular age. Even snakes have a better reputation.

Nigel Pickering, however, disagrees with all the demonisation. A former police diver from England, he came out to South Africa with his wife, Lesley, in 2003 and chose to live in the small and leafy town of Umkomaas, 25 miles south of Durban on the KwaZulu-Natal coast. Umkomaas is a quiet, amiable sort of place with a few good restaurants and bars on a long stretch of sandy shoreline. Nigel and Lesley set up their dive school in a handsome clapboard building with bright comfortable rooms for divers to stay in. There was, however, one other major attraction that drew Nigel to this coast: sharks. About four miles offshore, in the impressively muscular ocean, is a shallow area known as Aliwal Shoal. It is regularly listed among the world's top dive sites, being home to myriad sea creatures, including several species of shark. And Nigel is on a mission when it comes to sharks.

Diving with a ragged-tooth shark on Aliwal Shoal, South Africa. *Photograph: Alamy*

2 What is the TAP of this text?

Text type = _____

Audience = _____

Purpose = _____

Activity 3

10 minutes

Complete the table below by writing your own examples of a simple, complex, compound and minor sentence.

Simple sentence	Minor sentence	Compound sentence	Complex sentence
I feel terrified.	Terror!	I feel terrified and I can hardly believe what is before me.	I feel terrified because I can see several rows of shark's teeth.

Activity 4

1 What is the TAP of the answer required by the following exam-style question?

Describe a place that has made a strong impression on you, either positive or negative. Explain the reasons for your choice and convey a strong sense of that place to your reader. **(16 marks)**

Text type = _____

Audience = _a general reader/audience_ _____

Purpose = _____

2 Fill in the word bank below to support your writing to describe and entertain in relation to the text type, audience and purpose you identified above. This will form a plan for the Writing question.

Word bank of descriptive/sensory vocabulary to convey a sense of place

3 Now complete a five-point plan (see your work from Lesson 5F pages 39–41).

_____

_____

_____

_____

_____

_____

_____

4 Complete the question, using your plan and word bank.

Activity 5

Annotate your answer to Activity 4 to identify **three** different sentence types and **three** examples of engaging vocabulary.

Note down what you did well and areas for improvement.

Successes: _____

_____

Targets for improvement: _____

_____

Activity 6

10 minutes

Look at the following answer to the question in Activity 4, page 50. Annotate it with the improvements you would make to improve it.

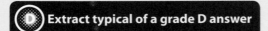
Extract typical of a grade D answer

> As the bold bright beautiful and laser beaming sun swiftly strolls beyond the foreground of my dark chocolate eyes. Comfortably lying down in the beach of Spana located near Spain. Nothing on my mind. Everything to do. I can expect others to do everything for me. I can just wish instead of do. Spain is where life begins!

Here and on the following page are extracts from two student responses to the question in Activity 4:

> Describe a place that has made a strong impression on you, either positive or negative. Explain the reasons for your choice and convey a strong sense of that place to your reader.
>
> (16 marks)

Read the answers together with the examiner comments. Match the examiner comments with the answers. Then complete the Tips and practice section on page 57.

Extract typical of a grade D answer

Student A

Rhyl

One place that has made an impression on me is Rhyl. It has also made an impression on my granddad as he's got a caravan there and he loves it.

Me, I don't get it. Lots of people have caravans there and go there for the weekend. We all stay there with my brothers and granddad and grandma. But we are all squashed in and you can hear everyone else through the cardboard walls. What is the point of even leaving your flat to go to somwhere just as small?

Round about it is no better. The beach at Rhyl you cant really call a beach. The sand is quiet brown and its more like sticky mud. Theres no way you'd sunbath on it. All we do it skim stones and there's a few birds to look at but mainly only seaguls. The town is grey and the view from the beach is a bit dull. There are a few houses with bords on the windows.

GradeStudio

Student B

> Awareness of audience and purpose establishing setting in relation to the title

> Words describing the men and women show developed vocabulary

The local park is a depressing place. It's meant to be a park for children and families and it's used by them in the day. Old men sit around chatting on park benches, moaning. Mums with lots of children sit on benches chatting and not really watching what their children are doing. And children are running round where there are bits of broken glass and equipments that have peeling paint and are not always working properly.

> Attempt to create atmosphere with additional descriptive detail

> Short simple sentence followed by minor and complex sentences provide variety

It's at night that the problems start. Shadows. Quiet spooky paths through the trees. Groups of teenagers from the community college sit in the children's playground where they are not allowed to be. It's the teenagers, drinking and playing on the equipment that's too small for them, that make problems that are left for the daytime. You can't walk through the park if you're not one of their gang without one of them shouting something at you.

> Minor sentence for effect

Examiner comment I

The student attempts to engage the reader with descriptive passages. Spelling is generally accurate but vocabulary lacks variety and interest. Sentence structures are generally secure but rely on simple and compound sentence structures.

Examiner comment 2

There are three different kinds of sentence here, all securely and accurately marked out. Vocabulary is reasonably varied and used consciously to create an atmosphere.

Student A matches examiner comment _____

Student B matches examiner comment _____

Tips and practice

Tips

Write down or discuss what you have learnt about:

Varying sentences _____

_____

Varying vocabulary _____

_____

Practice

Now apply what you have learnt to all your writing practice.

1 Check that you have used at least **one** of each form and are not relying on one sort of sentence type throughout your writing.

2 Create a word bank.

3 Check that you have used a variety of vocabulary linked to your audience and purpose.

Improving my responses

Now that you have completed this lesson using a range of vocabulary and sentence forms, fill in the RAG table below to see if your confidence has improved.

	R	A	G
I can consistently write in sentences that are complete and grammatically correct.	○	○	○
I understand the terms simple, complex, compound and minor sentences.	○	○	○
I can write in simple, complex, compound and minor sentences.	○	○	○
I can choose particular sentence types to achieve particular effects in my writing.	○	○	○
I can choose vocabulary to create particular effects in my writing.	○	○	○

Using a variety of punctuation

Skills you need:

You must show that you can:
- Understand how to use a full range of punctuation marks
- Use a range of punctuation marks in writing

Lots of you will know, in theory, how to use a variety of punctuation marks. Many students forget to demonstrate this to the examiner. Examiners can only mark what they see, so it's important that you show them the range of what you know. Many students tend to rely on full stops and commas to punctuate their work.

Once you have finished writing, proofread your work and check that you have demonstrated a few other punctuation marks. Beware of using too many of the same punctuation mark; for example, lots of students overuse the exclamation mark or write a whole descriptive piece using direct speech.

This lesson will revise how to use common punctuation marks. It will support you in practising how to use them.

Improving my responses

Fill in the RAG table below to show how confident you are in the following areas:

	R	A	G
I can use commas, full stops, question marks, ellipses and exclamation marks.	○	○	○
I can punctuate direct speech correctly.	○	○	○
I remember to use a variety of punctuation marks in my writing.	○	○	○

Activity 1

Fill in the table below to explain how you should use each punctuation mark.

Punctuation mark	Rules of use
Full stop •	
Inverted commas " "	
Comma ,	
Apostrophe ,	
Question mark ?	
Exclamation mark !	
Ellipsis • • •	

Activity 2

1 Look at this advert from the Autism Trust featuring the charity's founder,
   Polly Tommey.

Hello Boys.
Autism is worth
over 6 million votes.
It's time to talk ...

the
autism
trust

www.theautismtrust.org.uk

Polly Tommey

2 Identify the punctuation marks used in the advert and
   explain why they have been used.

1 Punctuation mark: _____

   Purpose: _____

   _____

2 Punctuation mark: _____

   Purpose: _____

   _____

3 Punctuation mark: _____

   Purpose: _____

   _____

Activity 3

15 minutes

1 Autism is a type of disability. People with autism find it difficult to communicate emotionally and understand what others think.
Read the Autism Trust press release which accompanied the advert shown in Activity 2.

Polly Tommey's Campaign Continues...
Labour Party first to respond.

Last week Polly Tommey sent letters to the three main party leaders urging them to talk to her about autism in the UK and the action needed. Yesterday the Labour Party responded with an invitation to discuss how they can help the autism community. Tomorrow, Polly will go to Downing Street to do just that.

Polly says, 'The Labour Party have not underestimated the power of the autism community. With over 6 million votes and the current likelihood of a hung parliament, it really is in the interest of the party leaders to come forward with some concrete policies to encourage our vote; we have the power to determine the general election outcome.'

Polly's billboards will be displayed from Monday 29th March in London's most viewed digital billboard locations, as well as multiple locations throughout the UK.

2 Write an alternative slogan for the campaign, using a variety of punctuation marks from Activity 1.

_____

_____

_____

_____

_____

_____

_____

Activity 4

1 Identify the TAP required by this exam question:

> **Write a letter of complaint or support to the Autism Trust in reaction to their ad campaign. Explain the reasons for your viewpoint and argue your case for or against.** **(16 marks)**

Hello Boys.
Autism is worth
over 6 million votes.
It's time to talk...

autism trust   www.theautismtrust.org.uk

Polly Tommey

Text type = _____

Audience = _____

Purpose = _____

2 Now answer the question, making sure you use at least **one** example of each of the punctuation marks discussed in Activity 1. You can tick them off in the list below.

Full stop		Question mark	
Inverted commas " "		Exclamation mark	
Comma		Ellipsis	
Apostrophe			

_____

_____

_____

_____

_____

_____

_____

Continue ▶

Continue ▶

Activity 5

Read the extract below. Annotate the answer to improve it by correcting the punctuation errors.

I am writing to support Polly Tommey and her brave work for

your autism advert what proves that she has done the right

thing is that the three leader's have all been in contact with her

to discuss autism as a result of the ad! I have a brother with

autism and knowing exactly the effect of this on the family and

the stress that people with the condition and their families

have and how there has not been enough attention given to this

issue. If the only way to get attention of the people in power is

to be provocative then why not, it's the twenty first century and

we don't live like Victorian's any more! As Polly herself said 'many

parent's of autistic children would take off their clothes and

run round the park naked if it got the attention of the people in

power to do something about this important issue!'

Here are extracts from two student responses to the question in Activity 4 page 62.

1 Read the answers together with the examiner comments.

Extract typical of a grade D answer

Student A

> Dear Ms Tommeee, I'm angry at the advert you used. It certainly gets attention but it sure aint what I'd expect in 2011.
> Why did you do it. I think this is more about showing off than making serious messages. It is bad enough putting up with this kind of thing in car adverts like the Renault one but not for a charity that should be helping todays young people. You should get real and take it that making a point can be done with serious words not just taking your clothes off.

Examiner comment

The candidate writes in a generally formal style, with a couple of lapses into informal English. Sentence structure is usually secure though punctuation lacks variety. The candidate relies on simple and compound sentences and needs to add a wider variety of sentence structure.

Extract typical of a grade C answer

Student B

> Dear Sir/Madam, I am writing about your billboard that I spotted today in London's Marble Arch. I must say I am very disturbed by your old fashioned views that are displayed there. Maybe you could say this is a joke, but after the hard work of women in previous generations, there is no excuse for using women's bodies for cheap political reasons!
> Cheap! Nasty! Low! These describe this advert! In future, please fight your battles through issues rather than by putting us down.
> What do you think you are playing at? This does us no favours. I, for one, will no longer be supporting your fundraising work.

Use of exclamation for effect

Use of exclamation mark – rather overused

Rhetorical question

Examiner comment

The candidate's work adopts an appropriate register for argument, though at times veers towards informal vocabulary and structures. A range of simple punctuation is used consciously for effect.

2 Now write down **five** examiner tips for students answering this question, before completing the Tips and practice section below.

- _____
- _____
- _____
- _____
- _____

Tips and practice

Tips

Write down or discuss what you have learnt about:

The rules of punctuation _____
_____

Using a variety of punctuation marks _____
_____

Practice

Now apply what you have learnt to all your writing practice.

1 Check that you have used a variety of punctuation marks and not overused any of the less common marks such as exclamation marks.

2 Read your work 'aloud in your head' to ensure that all sentences are correctly punctuated and make sense in themselves.

Improving my responses

Now that you have completed this lesson on using a variety of punctuation, fill in the RAG table below to see if your confidence has improved.

	R	A	G
I can use commas, full stops, question marks, ellipses and exclamation marks.	○	○	○
I can punctuate direct speech correctly.	○	○	○
I remember to use a variety of punctuation marks in my writing.	○	○	○

Skills you need:

You must show that you can:
- Recognise when a sentence is complete and grammatically correct
- Use a range of punctuation accurately
- Use a range of vocabulary with accurate spelling
- Recognise the importance of proofreading all written work

When it comes to the final exam, there are two skills that students often forget in the panic to write an answer: planning (covered in lesson 5F) and proofreading. No matter how well you have been taught English skills, if you fail to proofread your work, you are seriously risking your final grade.

Checking your work is not the most exciting part of writing. Getting my own students to read their work aloud often shows them writing material that does not make sense. On reading aloud, they are able to correct the majority of their mistakes, but they feel embarrassed that they have not seen the mistakes in the first place. Try to 'read aloud in your head' in the exam, to 'hear' what you have written.

This lesson allows you to practise your proofreading skills. It demonstrates some of the common mistakes students make. It supports you in planning time for proofreading in the final exam.

Improving my responses

Fill in the RAG table below to show how confident you are in the following areas:	R	A	G
I can recognise when sentences are secure or insecure.	○	○	○
I can use a range of punctuation accurately.	○	○	○
I can use a range of vocabulary that is accurately spelt.	○	○	○
I always proofread my written work.	○	○	○

Common problems with sentences

- Comma splicing: dividing sentences with a comma rather than a full stop or equivalent
  Barbados has unspoilt beaches and a lively nightlife, on the island you will find something for all the family.
- No finite verb
  Lying in the heat of the sun, the water lapping at my feet and a cocktail on the table next to me.

- Tense not maintained

  it was *the best holiday of my life and Eleanor* will *be able to come with me*

- Subject–verb agreement

  Our hotel, famous for its friendliness and charm, welcome *children and animals.*

- General sentence sense

  The animals, looking through the cages we all feeling like it, though knowing it's not right.

Activity 1

20 minutes

Read the sentences below. Highlight secure sentences in yellow. Highlight insecure sentences in pink. Annotate each with a reason for your decision. Rewrite the sentences that need improving in the spaces given.

It will be a dream holiday, firstly I attended all rides and have the time of my life.

_____

_____

In the side of the blue calm hot ocean, with the sandy sea side and the hot sun's reflection from the sand, was heard by the whales and smelt by my grandmother, it was tasted by the fish and touched by me, I found myself in Dubai.

_____

_____

Fun for all the family! This is certainly my experience of CentreParks.

_____

_____

Spain meant for him that there was no school, no homework, but also no stress. Just living his life to the best when he was there!

_____

_____

Sunbathing on the beach, the sound of the birds circling above the sea and the splash of the waves on the shoreline.

_____

_____

Activity 2

20 minutes

1 Imagine you are standing near this volcano. Make a word bank to describe what you can hear, smell, see and feel.

2 Now look at the following exam question:

> **Write a letter to your friend explaining why you would like him or her to join you on a trip to Stromboli, an island near Italy, to visit the volcano.** **(16 marks)**

Write the first **two** paragraphs in response to this question, using vocabulary from the word bank you have made.

Continue ▶

_____

_____

_____

_____

_____

_____

_____

_____

_____

_____

_____

_____

_____

_____

_____

_____

_____

3 Check your work against the success criteria below:
   - Do all sentences make sense? Are they grammatically correct? Are they punctuated?
   - Have you maintained a consistent tense, e.g. future tense in talking about the trip and present tense in describing the volcano and why it is interesting?
   - Have you checked spellings?
   - Have you used some interesting and engaging vocabulary?

4 Complete your response overleaf, remembering to check against the success criteria.

Continue ▶

Activity 3

10 minutes

1 Read the examination question below.

> **Write a letter of complaint from a package holiday tourist to his/her travel company for the disorganised reaction to the chaos caused by a volcanic eruption and the impact on his/her travel plans. Outline the problems that he/she encountered and suggest how the travel company should compensate for them.** **(16 marks)**

2 You are now going to proofread the opening section of a student's response to this question. Annotate the extract with any corrections you would suggest. Write out a best version of any sentences that need reworking above near the relevant sentence.

Dear Sirs, the volcano in Iceland has caused total chaos. We are stranded in

Malaga airport with two children and you haven't done a thing about it, we would

like to know what you are going to do and how u are going to help you.

The problems began last Thursday when our flight was cancelled because of the

volcano. Instead of you sorting out hotel arangments for our family had to find

you first and spend many euros making phone calls on an expensive mobile network

before we could even get any information from Happy Holidays. Booking our hotel

for another week This is what we should all expect. We have know spend another

week in Spain and needing to get home for work and school. Going by boat and

train, their is certainly other options. What are u going to do about this.

Activity 4

15 minutes

Proofread your completed response for Activity 2. List any suggestions for alterations that you would make as a result of what you have learnt from the proofreading exercise in Activity 3.

Suggestions for improvement:

_____

_____

_____

_____

_____

_____

_____

Re-read the exam question and answer in Activity 3, page 74.

Use the table below to check that you have identified and corrected examples of each of these points for improvement.

	Tick or cross
Sentence sense corrections	
Spelling corrections	
Language formality	

Read this examiner comment about the answer on page 74. Then complete the Tips and practice section that follows.

> **Examiner comment**
>
> There are several examples of sentences not making sense, either due to vocabulary, missing a finite verb or punctuation. As a result, sentence structures cannot be marked as 'secure'. Spelling is similar, with more than one example of spelling errors for words that sound similar but are spelt differently. A formal style is not maintained throughout.

Tips and practice

Tips

Write down or discuss what you have learnt about:

what to check when proofreading your writing: _____

_____

_____

_____

Practice

Now apply what you have learnt to all your writing practice.

1 TAP your examination question.
2 Ensure that you have used the correct language, paragraphing, sentence structures and form to reflect your text type, audience and purpose.
3 Ensure that you have used a variety of vocabulary, punctuation and paragraph lengths to convey your ideas.

Improving my responses

Now that you have completed this lesson on proofreading, fill in the RAG table below to see if your confidence has improved.

	R	A	G
I can recognise when sentences are secure or insecure.	◯	◯	◯
I can use a range of punctuation accurately.	◯	◯	◯
I can use a range of vocabulary that is accurately spelt.	◯	◯	◯
I always proofread my written work.	◯	◯	◯

Skills you need:

You must show that you can:

- Identify the text type, audience and purpose (TAP) of a Writing question
- Choose the form of your writing and demonstrate its features
- Use an appropriate register

You will answer **two** Writing questions in the AQA GCSE English exam.

In order to 'communicate effectively' you need to identify exactly **who** you are writing for, what **form** the writing should take and what **features** of writing you need to display in that form. For example, an exam question may ask you to write for people your own age, the form might be a magazine article and the features you will then need to display are presentational (for example, subheadings and headings). You can use the TAP technique (text type, audience, purpose) that you are already familiar with in your Reading work before planning a Writing answer.

Think carefully about the kind of language you should use for the topic. Consider whether you should write informally or formally (the register). Beware of writing very informally. Avoid slipping into text speak and slang, even if the exam question encourages you to write informally. You still need to display your command of the English language.

This lesson will help you to pinpoint exactly what a question is asking you to do and identify the features you must use to gain the best marks possible.

Improving my responses

Fill in the RAG table below to show how confident you are in the following areas:	R	A	G
I can identify the text type, audience and purpose required of a Writing exam question.	○	○	○
I can write in a variety of forms and include their appropriate presentational, structural and language features.	○	○	○
I can identify an appropriate register (when to write formally and when to write informally).	○	○	○

Activity 1

10 minutes

Choose **three** of the text types below and list the features you would expect to find in them. The first one has been done for you.

informal letter	formal letter	
report	leaflet	newspaper article
speech	review	magazine article

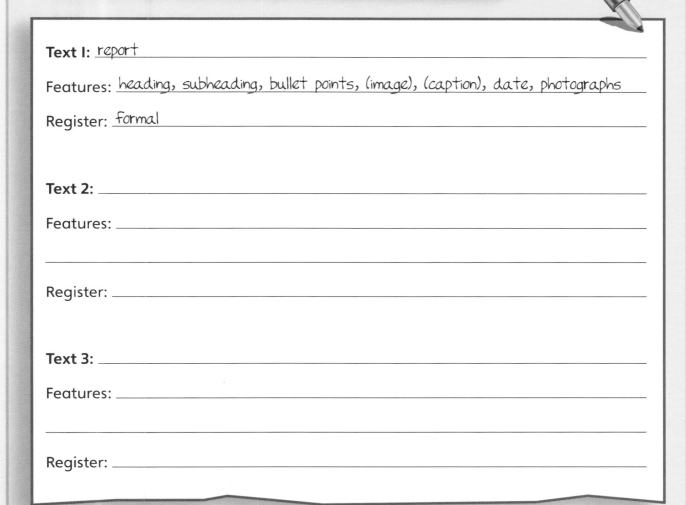

Text 1: report

Features: heading, subheading, bullet points, (image), (caption), date, photographs

Register: formal

Text 2: _____

Features: _____

_____

Register: _____

Text 3: _____

Features: _____

_____

Register: _____

Activity 2

15 minutes

1 Identify the TAP, register and structural features of the following exam question:

> **Write a front page newspaper article for the local newspaper, the *Witney Gazette*, about a charity fire-walking event.**
>
> **You might write about:**
> * **when and where the event took place**
> * **participants' reasons for taking part**
> * **a description of the spectacle of the actual event.**   **(24 marks)**

Text type = _____

Audience = _____

Purpose = _____

Register (formal/informal) = _____

Structural features = _____

_____

_____

_____

2 In order to write your newspaper article, read the following transcript of a video about the fire walking event. Underline any details that you think might be useful to include in your writing.

The Fire Walkers of Witney

11 March 2010 ... A group of brave individuals take of their shoes and socks and walk on a 20ft-long bed of burning wood for charity.

37 volunteers removed their shoes and socks for a charity fire walk in Witney town square...

Participant 1: I'm really looking forward to it. We're all pretty charged up so it should be good.

Interviewer: How charged up?

Participant 1: I dunno, pretty charged up. We all pretty charged up? Yeah, pretty good.

Interviewer: What attracted you to do fire walking?

Participant 2: I have no idea. It was his fault.

Interviewer: Why do you want to do it?

Vicar 1: Well, I just want to raise a lot of money for a good cause, really. I mean Helen and Douglas House is a really really worthwhile charity and we should just give as much as we can to them.

Vicar 2: Well we're gonna do this fire walk and I'm gonna do it because Toby told me I had to do it. He came to us and he said we're gonna ... three clergyman who are trustees of base 33, have to do this fire walk. He didn't give me any choice. He didn't ask me, he just said you're gonna do it.

Interviewer: What about you, sir?

Vicar 3: Well I'm doing it for base 33, for the young people. So, I think that's it really ... I wouldn't do it otherwise. It's absolute insanity, madness.

Interviewer: Does this fire walk have an ecclesiastical sort of ring to it?

Vicar 4: Well, ur, there are people who said to me that it's a bit pagan, but actually if we look into the Old Testament we see Shadrach, Meshach and Abednego go wandering in that and apparently some monks in islands off Greece have been doing this as a spiritual discipline in order to bring them nearer to God as well, so I don't think there's a problem there.

Interviewer: You're not going down that route, you're just gonna do it for a good cause.

Participant 3: Just doing it for a good cause, good night out and I hope lots of fun.

Participant 4: I've always been interested in this and um I just thought, well, now's the moment. You know, I'm getting on a bit, now's my chance.

Interviewer: How many times have you walked on the fire?

Organiser 1: [laughter] err, we take it in turns so probably about 500 times. At least.

Interviewer: And you've never burned your feet?

Organiser 1: No. I wouldn't do it again if I had.

Organiser 2: We've been doing this for 26 years now. We have no injuries, no accidents, no incidents of any kind. What we like to do is come along, do our fire walking, and leave people behind with happy faces and mucky feet. That's what we like and lots of money raised for the causes close to their heart.

Participant 5: It's gonna be really good. We're gonna have a really good session with um Karen here um who will get us all in the frame of mind where we're actually able to take that first step to walk the 20 feet along the fire track.

[band plays and fire walk is prepared]
[claps and cheers]

MC: Listen, guys. First of all I'd like to say please do not try this at home for obvious reasons. These guys have been trained up to do this for the last 2 hours. All I'm asking for you is if you could give each and every one of them the biggest Jerry Springer round of applause. Thank you very much!

[claps and cheers as each participant fire walks]

Participant 3: That's been a fantastic evening, absolutely wonderful. Such fun, and just amazing that everyone went through with it, and 100% success and ... absolutely tremendous and wonderful to watch the confidence of people as they got ready for it and prepared for it, went outside, saw the fire and then got going and walked across it. Absolutely tremendous.

Activity 3

Complete your newspaper article in answer to the question in Activity 2, page 80 using the template below.

> **Write a front page newspaper article for the local newspaper, the *Witney Gazette*, about a charity fire-walking event.**
>
> **You might write about:**
> • **when and where the event took place**
> • **participants' reasons for taking part**
> • **a description of the spectacle of the actual event.**
>
> **(24 marks)**

Witney Gazette

Continue ▶

Continue ▶

Activity 4

Read the sample opening below, along with the C grade criteria. What improvements can be made to the answer?

Witney Gazette

Witney fire walkers

On 11th March some of our local people braved fire and walked over burning wood. Would you? The band played music and a crowd of locals turned up to watch. Why did they do this? 37 people walked across the fire and they raised money for charity.

- The people involved in the fire walking were charged up.
- There were saftey people there, but the people running the entertainment said they there was no chance of an accident with this event.

- The event was good and 2500 quid was raised for charite.

C

▶ Engages the local reader with descriptive detail and factual information

▶ Writes a formal newspaper article, the tone and language of which is appropriately serious

▶ Employs short paragraphs and simple sentence structures appropriate for the newspaper form

▶ Uses a variety of structural features, e.g. different paragraph lengths, direct and reported speech, headline and subheads

▶ Uses a range of interesting and relevant vocabulary

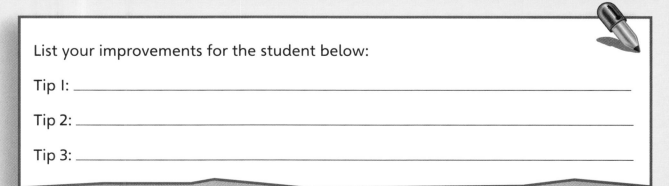

List your improvements for the student below:

Tip 1: _____

Tip 2: _____

Tip 3: _____

GradeStudio

Here are extracts from two student responses to the following exam question:

> Write a national newspaper article front page story to go out on 1st April.
> In the tradition of past April Fool stories, the form and language will need to convince the readers of the truth of the April Fool's joke.
>
> (16 marks)

Read the answers together with the examiner comments, before completing the Tips and practice section on page 85.

Extract typical of a grade D answer

Student A

The Education Minster announced today that schools will now be run by MI5, the Uk's Securite Service. Hot on the heels of his rule that teachers will now be recruited from the army, Mi5 have Said they think their the best people to do the job. The head of MI5 said We will be able to get the best grades possible for pupils. We can also quickly spot pupils who are not fitting in to expectations of behaviour and attendance. We are the ones to deal with them.

Examiner comment

- Factual details given.
- Direct speech used.
- Shorter sentences and paragraphs needed for a tabloid newspaper.
- Engages the reader with amusing storyline.
- Errors in spelling and punctuation.

Extract typical of a grade C answer

Student B

The education Minister announced today that all students will be given porridge before starting lessons in school. This will be a compulsory part of the school day and will give everyone a good start.

"It's been good enough for me for years and has got me where I am today. Porridge is a nutritous and wholesome food. Too many children today are going to school without a good breakfast and this is one reason for underachevement,' he told teachers at Wildon High school, during a visit this morning.

Jamie Oliver, celebrity chef, has supported this move. He has suggested he will be publishing a booklet for schools of exciting new porridge recipes for today's students.

Examiner comment

- Engaging, amusing story to interest readers.
- Appropriate factual information included.
- Short paragraphs and simple sentence structures appropriate for tabloid format.
- Uses a range of interesting vocabulary.
- Generally accurate spelling and punctuation.

Tips and practice

Tips

Write down or discuss what you have learnt about:

TAPping your question _____

_____

Writing in a particular form _____

_____

Practice

Now apply what you have learnt to all your writing practice.

1 TAP your exam question.
2 Ensure you have used the correct language, paragraphing, sentence structures and form to reflect your text type, audience and purpose.
3 Ensure that you have used a variety of vocabulary, punctuation and paragraph lengths to convey your ideas.

Improving my responses

Now that you have completed this lesson on writing to communicate effectively, fill in the RAG table below to see if your confidence has improved.

	R	A	G
I can identify the text type, audience and purpose required of a Writing exam question.	○	○	○
I can write in a variety of forms and demonstrate their appropriate presentational, structural and language features.	○	○	○
I can identify an appropriate register (when to write formally and when to write informally).	○	○	○

10F Approaching the exam paper

Now you have completed these revision lessons you have revisited the AQA GCSE English skills you learnt during your English course. Part of your success in the exam lies in your **knowledge** of these English skills. Another part lies in your **application** of these skills, together with your **exam technique**. Now it is time to apply your skills to the exam papers.

Throughout the revision lessons you have addressed English skills and collected exam tips from the materials and your teacher. This section brings everything together.

Part I checks on your exam technique. You will then apply your English skills to the exam-style questions in Part 2.

Part 1: exam technique

Look at the exam questions that follow on pages 89–95. They have all been annotated with things you need to think about when answering these types of questions.

Do not answer the exam questions themselves, but use the boxes provided to make notes in answer to the annotations on *how* you would approach the questions.

Read **Item 1 'Suits under scrutiny'** and answer the questions below.

> What do you need to identify about this article before you begin work on it?

> Which are the key words in the question you would underline?

1 List 4 things the article tells you about how *Which?* tested the quality of suits.

> Which sections of the source text will you underline?

(4 marks)

> How long should you spend on this question?

> Which sections of the source text will you underline?

2 Why do *Which?* magazine authors think that their readers will be particularly interested in this topic?

> Will you use quotations in your answer?

(4 marks)

> How long should you spend on this question?

> Approximately how many separate points will you make in answer to this question?

Item 1

which **?**

Suits
under scrutiny

We investigate cut price ladies' suits to see if you really can bag a bargain for less than £60...

Women's clothing

Looking sharp for a job interview when you're on a budget can be a challenge – but our snapshot look at recession busting ladies' suits saw New Look triumph in the style stakes. A £32 New Look suit came top in our quest to find a good quality interview suit beating outfits from Asda, Tesco, Debenhams and Matalan.

Suit selection

We bought the cheapest black trouser suit from five high street retailers offering low-cost suits. All cost less than £60 – and some were less than £20.

We removed all labels and asked expert tailor Eddie Rowland from Redwood and Feller in London to assess the suits for cut, shape, presentation and fabric.

Expert views

Our expert thought that while most of the garments represented good value for money, none would last well after repeated wear and cleaning. The most expensive suit, a Debenhams version made from recycled plastic bottles was deemed 'poor', with our expert commenting, 'It's a clever idea but the workmanship seems to be lacking'. Many suits had hanging threads, poorly attached buttons, unmatched fastenings and rough seams.

One – a £23 suit from Matalan – even had a sleeve that appeared to have been attached the wrong way round. This suit earned the lowest score – our expert pointed out uncoordinated fastenings, loose buttons and prominent stitching.

New Look's suit gained the highest score. Our expert said, 'Immediately you can see the presentation seems a lot cleaner than the rest – they've finished the darts off nicely and the cut is better'.

What do you need to identify about this article before you begin work on it?

Now read **Item 2 'Renault's cool wind of change'** on page 92 and answer the question below.

Which are the key words in the question you would underline?

3 What evidence can you find in the article that the car is both recommended and criticised?

Which sections of the source text will you underline?

Will you use quotations in your answer?

Recommendations

Criticisms

How long should you spend on this question?

Approximately how many separate points will you make in answer to this question?

(8 marks)

Item 2

Renault's cool wind of change

WE'LL start with the obvious. Yes, this funky, cool-looking new two-seater roadster from Renault has just about the most unfunkiest and uncoolest name you could possibly ever imagine. Ladies and gentlemen, this is the new Renault Wind.

Despite what could very well turn out to be one of the trendiest cars introduced this year the French firm has given it a name that could make it the laughing stock of the car park. Successful cars have coped with odd names before of course, VW's Sharan and Nissan's Qashqai most recently, but nothing to quite suggest a bodily function that has small children doubling up with the giggles.

Given that car firms pay small fortunes to specialist agencies to come up with suitably neutral and worldwide-friendly names it's nothing short of a staggering own goal. Will we see a Whoopee Cushion limited edition version?

It's also a huge shame because there's no question that many potential owners will be put off by the baby Renault's name alone and not discover that the Wind is actually one of the best cars we've driven this year.

It certainly looks the part. Petite, stylish and elegant the Wind manages to be a good-looking car in a sector that's dominated by, well, rather feminine-looking choices.

It's no secret that the likes of the Mini convertible and Mazda MX-5 tend to attract more female buyers (despite their respective driving talents) but the Wind manages to look like a miniature supercar with the Jaguar XJS-style sleek buttresses and sporty rear end. It's a design that's pleasing to the eye whatever your sex.

Also, unlike the Mini drop-top, the Renault manages this feat of styling while also linked to a folding hard-top roof, usually a sure-fire guarantee of ugliness due to packaging issues.

In fact the Wind's roof doesn't actually fold but cleverly flips up and over in one section, pivoting around the roll-over hoop just behind the head of the two front passengers and into a hollow in the boot lid.

Convertible purists might claim this makes the car more of a targa, like the old Porsche 911 or Toyota MR2 but the fact remains that the conversion from closed to alfresco is quick and easy via a twist grip just above the rear-view mirror and then a button on the lower dashboard.

Better yet it also doesn't harm the Wind's practicality either, more of which later.

Renault claims three-quarters of all small drop-top sales are cars with small engines, so the Wind will be offered with a choice of only two petrol engines: a 100bhp 1.2-litre turbo and a 1.6 with 133bhp.

Despite those sporty looks though, neither is especially rapid. The 1.2 manages the 0 to 60mph sprint in 10.5 seconds together with a 118mph top speed, while the 1.6 isn't much faster at 9.2 seconds and 125mph respectively. But both manage average fuel economies of more than 40mpg.

Better still there's also a well-built and smart interior. For a car that's aimed at such a fun and youthful end of the market it could possibly be a bit more interesting inside design-wise, apart from a translucent coloured plastic cowl over the dials, it can't rival the trendier Citroën DS3 or Mini.

We'd also like to have had reach adjustment on the steering wheel rather than just height, which can make for a slightly awkward driving position for taller drivers.

On the practicality side though, the Wind scores full points with sizeable door pockets and a huge boot whether the roof is up or down.

With a starting price of £15,500, the Wind is very competitively priced, especially so when you consider the long list of standard equipment which includes alloy wheels, air-conditioning and electric windows together with that electric roof.

However the baby Renault's most crucial piece of equipment can't be found on the spec sheet: it's the feeling you get behind the wheel during even the shortest of drives.

The Wind isn't perfect but above all else it's fun and at this price it offers unbeatable smiles per mile, something that's too often lacking at modern accountant-run car manufacturers.

If we drive a better value drop-top this year we'll eat our hats. All you need to do is ignore that name.

Read **Item 3 'Green Gym – Chipping Norton'** on page 94 and answer the question below.

4 How does the writer use language to make the leaflet informative and persuasive to the reader?

> What do you need to identify about this article before you begin work on it?

> Will you use quotations in your answer?

> Will you comment on the pictures in the leaflet?

> Which are the key words in the question you would underline?

Informative

> Which sections of the source text will you underline?

Persuasive

> Which sections of the source text will you underline?

(12 marks)

> How long should you spend on this question?

> Approximately how many separate points will you make in answer to this question?

Item 3

Green Gym – Chipping Norton

What is the BTCV Green Gym?

BTCV Green Gym is a unique scheme to help you become physically and mentally healthier by taking part in nature conservation activities to improve your local environment such as

→ Tree planting

→ Woodland management

→ Creating wildflower gardens

→ Hedge laying

BTCV Green gym offers a new way to get fit, healthy and a great way to become physically active in an outdoor environment.

Participating in the BTCV Green Gym, surrounded by green open space, is a refreshing way to reduce stress levels and improve any participant's overall mental and emotional health.

Who's who

The BTCV Gym in Chipping Norton has been created in partnership with West Oxfordshire District Council and LEADER+ and is supported by the Wychwood Project. Based on sites in Chipping Norton and the surrounding area, the BTCV gym will provide opportunities for local residents and community groups to get involved with gardening and practical conservation activities.

BTCV Green Gym in Chipping Norton is striving to work with local health service providers to provide an alternative to conventional exercise and therapeutic schemes, helping to improve West Oxfordshire's physical and mevntal health, and the environment at the same time.

BTCV Green Gym has been independently evaluated by the Healthcare research and development Department of Oxford Brookes University.

5 Now look again at all 3 items on pages 90, 92 and opposite.
  They have each been presented in an interesting and effective way.

  Choose 2 of these items. Compare them using these headings:
  • the titles and subtitles
  • the pictures and captions.

Which are the key words in the question you would underline?

Which two will you choose and why?

How long should you spend on this question?

Will you use quotations in your answer?

What kind of planning format(s) will you use to compare and contrast before writing?

(12 marks)

Part 2: applying English skills to exam questions

You are now going to build on this preparation and the work you have completed in exam technique by writing full, exam-style answers in timed conditions.

Section A: Reading

Answer **all** questions

You are advised to spend about one hour on this section.

Read **Item 1 'Suits under scrutiny'** and answer the questions below.

1a) List 4 things the article tells you about how *Which?* tested the quality of suits.

1 _____

2 _____

3 _____

4 _____

(4 marks)

1b) Why do *Which?* magazine authors think that their readers will be particularly interested in this topic?

_____

_____

_____

_____

_____

_____

_____

_____

_____

(4 marks)

Item 1

which **?**

Suits
under scrutiny

We investigate cut price ladies' suits to see if you really can bag a bargain for less than £60...

Women's clothing

Looking sharp for a job interview when you're on a budget can be a challenge – but our snapshot look at recession busting ladies' suits saw New Look triumph in the style stakes. A £32 New Look suit came top in our quest to find a good quality interview suit beating outfits from Asda, Tesco, Debenhams and Matalan.

Suit selection

We bought the cheapest black trouser suit from five high street retailers offering low-cost suits. All cost less than £60 – and some were less than £20.

We removed all labels and asked expert tailor Eddie Rowland from Redwood and Feller in London to assess the suits for cut, shape, presentation and fabric.

Expert views

Our expert thought that while most of the garments represented good value for money, none would last well after repeated wear and cleaning. The most expensive suit, a Debenhams version made from recycled plastic bottles was deemed 'poor', with our expert commenting, 'It's a clever idea but the workmanship seems to be lacking'. Many suits had hanging threads, poorly attached buttons, unmatched fastenings and rough seams.

One – a £23 suit from Matalan – even had a sleeve that appeared to have been attached the wrong way round. This suit earned the lowest score – our expert pointed out uncoordinated fastenings, loose buttons and prominent stitching.

New Look's suit gained the highest score. Our expert said, 'Immediately you can see the presentation seems a lot cleaner than the rest – they've finished the darts off nicely and the cut is better'.

Now read **Item 2 'Renaut's cool wind of change'** and answer the question below.

2 What evidence can you find in the article that the car is recommended, despite some criticisms. *(8 marks)*

_____

_____

_____

_____

_____

_____

_____

_____

_____

_____

_____

_____

_____

_____

_____

_____

_____

_____

_____

_____

_____

Item 2

Renault's cool wind of change

WE'LL start with the obvious. Yes, this funky, cool-looking new two-seater roadster from Renault has just about the most unfunkiest and uncoolest name you could possibly ever imagine. Ladies and gentlemen, this is the new Renault Wind.

Despite what could very well turn out to be one of the trendiest cars introduced this year the French firm has given it a name that could make it the laughing stock of the car park. Successful cars have coped with odd names before of course, VW's Sharan and Nissan's Qashqai most recently, but nothing to quite suggest a bodily function that has small children doubling up with the giggles.

Given that car firms pay small fortunes to specialist agencies to come up with suitably neutral and worldwide-friendly names it's nothing short of a staggering own goal. Will we see a Whoopee Cushion limited edition version?

It's also a huge shame because there's no question that many potential owners will be put off by the baby Renault's name alone and not discover that the Wind is actually one of the best cars we've driven this year.

It certainly looks the part. Petite, stylish and elegant the Wind manages to be a good-looking car in a sector that's dominated by, well, rather feminine-looking choices.

It's no secret that the likes of the Mini convertible and Mazda MX-5 tend to attract more female buyers (despite their respective driving talents) but the Wind manages to look like a miniature supercar with the Jaguar XJS-style sleek buttresses and sporty rear end. It's a design that's pleasing to the eye whatever your sex.

Also, unlike the Mini drop-top, the Renault manages this feat of styling while also linked to a folding hard-top roof, usually a sure-fire guarantee of ugliness due to packaging issues.

In fact the Wind's roof doesn't actually fold but cleverly flips up and over in one section, pivoting around the roll-over hoop just behind the head of the two front passengers and into a hollow in the boot lid.

Convertible purists might claim this makes the car more of a targa, like the old Porsche 911 or Toyota MR2 but the fact remains that the conversion from closed to alfresco is quick and easy via a twist grip just above the rear-view mirror and then a button on the lower dashboard.

Better yet it also doesn't harm the Wind's practicality either, more of which later.

Renault claims three-quarters of all small drop-top sales are cars with small engines, so the Wind will be offered with a choice of only two petrol engines: a 100bhp 1.2-litre turbo and a 1.6 with 133bhp.

Despite those sporty looks though, neither is especially rapid. The 1.2 manages the 0 to 60mph sprint in 10.5 seconds together with a 118mph top speed, while the 1.6 isn't much faster at 9.2 seconds and 125mph respectively. But both manage average fuel economies of more than 40mpg.

Better still there's also a well-built and smart interior. For a car that's aimed at such a fun and youthful end of the market it could possibly be a bit more interesting inside design-wise, apart from a translucent coloured plastic cowl over the dials, it can't rival the trendier Citroën DS3 or Mini.

We'd also like to have had reach adjustment on the steering wheel rather than just height, which can make for a slightly awkward driving position for taller drivers.

On the practicality side though, the Wind scores full points with sizeable door pockets and a huge boot whether the roof is up or down.

With a starting price of £15,500, the Wind is very competitively priced, especially so when you consider the long list of standard equipment which includes alloy wheels, air-conditioning and electric windows together with that electric roof.

However the baby Renault's most crucial piece of equipment can't be found on the spec sheet: it's the feeling you get behind the wheel during even the shortest of drives.

The Wind isn't perfect but above all else it's fun and at this price it offers unbeatable smiles per mile, something that's too often lacking at modern accountant-run car manufacturers. If we drive a better value drop-top this year we'll eat our hats. All you need to do is ignore that name.

Read **Item 3 'Green Gym – Chipping Norton'** and answer the question below.

3 How does the writer use language to make the leaflet informative and persuasive to the reader?   *(12 marks)*

_____

_____

_____

_____

_____

_____

_____

_____

_____

_____

_____

_____

_____

_____

_____

_____

_____

_____

_____

_____

_____

Item 3

Green Gym – Chipping Norton

What is the BTCV Green Gym?

BTCV Green Gym is a unique scheme to help you become physically and mentally healthier by taking part in nature conservation activities to improve your local environment such as

→ Tree planting

→ Woodland management

→ Creating wildflower gardens

→ Hedge laying

BTCV Green gym offers a new way to get fit, healthy and a great way to become physically active in an outdoor environment.

Participating in the BTCV Green Gym, surrounded by green open space, is a refreshing way to reduce stress levels and improve any participant's overall mental and emotional health.

Who's who

The BTCV Gym in Chipping Norton has been created in partnership with West Oxfordshire District Council and LEADER+ and is supported by the Wychwood Project. Based on sites in Chipping Norton and the surrounding area, the BTCV gym will provide opportunities for local residents and community groups to get involved with gardening and practical conservation activities.

BTCV Green Gym in Chipping Norton is striving to work with local health service providers to provide an alternative to conventional exercise and therapeutic schemes, helping to improve West Oxfordshire's physical and mevntal health, and the environment at the same time.

BTCV Green Gym has been independently evaluated by the Healthcare research and development Department of Oxford Brookes University.

4 Now look again at all 3 items. They have each been presented in an interesting and effective way.

Choose 2 of these items. Compare them using these headings:

- the titles and subtitles
- the pictures and captions.

(12 marks)

Section B: Writing

Answer **both** questions in this section.

You are advised to spend about one hour on this section.

1 Imagine that you are looking for a holiday job in one of your local clothes shops. Write a letter to the store manager, outlining your suitability for a job and explaining why you want to work there.   *(16 marks)*

_____

_____

_____

_____

_____

_____

_____

2 Imagine you have taken part in a sports or outdoor activity during the school holidays. Write a magazine article for a school or college newspaper recommending the activity to other students.

The article should include:
• information about the activity
• personal feedback on your own experience
• reasons why they should try the activity themselves.   *(24 marks)*

_____

_____

_____

_____

_____

_____

_____

_____

_____

_____

_____

Personal notes and reminders

You may want to use this page to write down your personal revision targets, as well as any useful hints and tips you have learnt during your revision lessons to make your revision successful.

_____

_____

_____

_____

_____

_____

_____

_____

_____

_____

_____

_____

_____

_____

_____

_____

_____

_____

_____

_____